Unbeaten

KIM WOODBURN

Unbeaten

The story of my brutal childhood

With Richard Barber

HODDER &
STOUGHTON

Names have been changed to protect identities.

First published in Great Britain in 2006 by Hodder & Stoughton
A division of Hodder Headline

This paperback edition published in 2007

A Hodder & Stoughton Book

1

A CIP catalogue record for this book is available
from the British Library

ISBN 9781444704334

Typeset in Plantin Light by M Rules
Printed and bound in the UK by CPI Mackays, Chatham ME5 8TD

Hodder Headline's policy is to use papers that are natural, renewable and recyclable products and made from wood grown in sustainable forests. The logging and manufacturing processes are expected to conform to the environmental regulations of the country of origin.

Hodder & Stoughton
A division of Hodder Headline
338 Euston Road
London NW1 3BH

To my lovely Uncle Neville and Auntie Pat.
Thank you very much for always being there
for me; you were the only ones who
always had an open door.
All my love, Kim

And with thanks to Luigi Bonomi,
my agent, and everyone at Hodder.
You have all been wonderful.

Contents

I

The Wicked Witch Is Dead

The letter arrived without warning.

It was mid-April 2000. My husband, Peter, and I were working as houseman and housekeeper for a German industrialist – one of the kindest of all our many employers – in a beautiful mansion in London's Belgravia. The letter was from my half-brother, Richard, someone I hadn't seen for almost twenty years – the last occasion, in fact, that I'd also seen my mother. 'Dear Sister,' it began, 'I write to tell you our mother died on April 11.' He went on to give the details of where and when she was to be buried, and the time the funeral party would be leaving the house in Portsmouth.

I'd always said that, when my mother died, I wouldn't go to her funeral. Reading the news of her death, I felt nothing, absolutely nothing. My mother was an evil, vicious woman who'd starved me of love throughout my childhood and beaten me mercilessly until, finally, I'd run away from home aged fifteen. When she must have known she was dying, she never got in touch with me, never felt the need to apologise for all the sadness and hurt, the neglect, that have affected me all my life. In the circumstances, perhaps I shouldn't have been surprised. What had I honestly expected?

But, for all that, there was something in me that made me feel I ought to attend her funeral. She'd carried me in her womb. The least I could do was to be there when she was put in the ground. I'm a decent human being, and I wanted some respect for myself. She may have behaved as she did, but I was her daughter and I needed to know I'd done the right thing by her.

I also thought that, as Richard had gone to the trouble to find out where I lived so he could give me the news, I should repay that decency. He'd been brought up by his grandparents in Sunderland so that we were virtual strangers to each other – he was nineteen the first time we met – but maybe he'd found out how badly I'd been treated by our mother. He himself had not known a mother's love – perhaps that was why he understood. Attending her send-off would be my way of thanking him for acknowledging me and what I'd been through. Little did I know what lay ahead.

The night before the funeral, Pete and I drove down to Portsmouth and booked in at a little B&B.

We called at the funeral parlour, then went round to the flat of my full sister, Gloria – but she wasn't there. As she'd assured us she would be in, I almost knocked her front door down for fear she hadn't heard us. Heaven knows where she was. But Gloria has always run by her own rules so we gave that up as a bad job. It was raining hard by then and we decided to call it a night.

Next morning Pete and I got to my mother's house at nine o'clock, about fifteen minutes before the cortege was due to leave for the church. It was Richard who opened the door, although it had been so long that I didn't immediately recognise him. He was friendly enough as we chatted in the hall. But as soon as we walked into the lounge the atmosphere became totally hostile. I recognised Robert, my eldest half-brother (or maybe my only full brother – no one knows), who was there with his own son, looking the spitting image of Robert at the same age. Then there was another half-brother, Neil, and my half-sisters Rosemary, Caroline and Janet. Pete and I found a couple of chairs and sat down. No one said a single word of greeting. No one offered us a cup of tea. It was chilling. What had our mother said about me behind my back? I could only guess.

There was also an old man there, someone I'd never seen before. He turned out to have been a scoutmaster the family had known for a long time, although only since I'd left home. He approached me.

'Excuse me, love,' he said. 'But who are you?'

So I told him I was my mother's second child. Not one member of the family spoke – they just shot me more filthy looks.

'I've known the family for years,' he said in obvious surprise, 'and your mother never mentioned you.'

I repeated that I was Gloria's younger sister.

'I didn't know she had one,' he said.

After that, Pete and I sat in silence, entirely ignored by everyone.

When it was time to leave for the service, after the longest quarter of an hour of my life, Pete and I followed in our car. My mother's coffin was waiting in the hearse when we got to the church. Gloria arrived at the same time with her daughter and two sons. Pete and I sat with them at the back of the church; all the half-brothers and -sisters sat at the front. Another half-sister, Penny, who'd been caught in traffic, had also gone straight to the church. There was no one else there – but then, my mother didn't have any friends.

The coffin was carried in by my half-brothers Rob, Richard and Neil, and by Rob's son. Richard then sat on his own at the front, sobbing silently, his face cupped in his hands. The rest of them remained dry-eyed. I was so upset at that stage by the way I'd been cold-shouldered that I find it hard now to remember every detail. I can't even recall whether there were flowers in the church. So intent was I on getting through what lay ahead that I was half-blind to what was going on around me.

What I do recollect very clearly indeed is what was – and was not – said. The priest stood up at the front and explained why we were all there. 'We are here to recall the life of Patricia Mary McGinley,' he began. 'She was christened Mary Patricia, but she didn't like the name Mary so she always called herself Pat. On behalf of her children, Gloria, Robert, Richard, Neil, Penny, Rosemary, Caroline and Janet, as well as the daughter she lost, Rose . . . all of them wish to remember their mother.'

I hadn't heard *my* name, and a feeling of deep, deep hurt ran through me. She couldn't do that to me. She couldn't. Who could disown their own child?

Pete turned to me and put his hand on mine. 'Did you hear your name?' he said.

I shook my head.

He asked if I wanted him to get up and say something.

'No,' I said. 'Leave it.' I felt completely numb.

Then my youngest half-sister, Janet, was walking to the front to say a few words – and once again I forced myself to concentrate on getting through this ordeal. 'Our mother was not the most tolerant of people,' I heard her saying. 'Our mother was prone to very bad moods. But she was our mother.' I could hardly believe my ears. Whatever I may have felt about my mother, every instinct told me that, if you can't say something nice about a person on an occasion like this, you don't say anything at all. Throughout my childhood I'd prayed and prayed for someone to rescue me from my mother and the grim, brutal life I was forced to live. For all that, though, Janet's remarks were inappropriate at a funeral. To me, silence would have been preferable.

Janet was still talking. 'The one thing our mother taught us girls,' she said, 'was to have smart hair and well-manicured nails.' How sad. Smart hair? Nice nails? That's some legacy, isn't it? What she should have left her children was a legacy of love and respect, the memory of what a good mum she'd been. *God help us!* I thought.

Then Neil got to his feet. 'Our mother was very volatile,' he began. 'She could be extremely fiery.' And on it went. I looked round at them all and still not one of them, with the single exception of Richard, was shedding a tear. Nobody seemed to be feeling any sense of grief that she'd gone. They were all sitting bolt upright and from where I was sitting, it seemed that they were doing little more than going through the motions.

At the end of the service, the priest spoke for the last time. 'Pat's children are gathered here today to say goodbye to their mother,' he said. And then came the final twist of the knife as he listed them again – and again of course, without mentioning me. It was as though I was a stranger on this earth, as though I didn't exist. It felt like my birthright had been taken from me.

It's clear to me now that this was my mother's final spiteful act. She was disowning me from beyond the grave. Out of all of them, I was the only one who'd never been prepared to take my mother's nonsense, who'd rebelled against her. And this was her ultimate act of revenge.

As we all filed out everyone continued to ignore me. I climbed into our car and finally – alone with Pete at last – I broke down.

'Do you want to go to the burial?' he asked.

But after what I'd just been through, I couldn't face that. 'I can't do it, Pete,' I replied.

'Come on then, love,' he said. 'Let's go home.'

I would have told you that, at fifty-eight years of age as I then was, I couldn't have been hurt deeply any more. Now, I know different. It was as if all the years in between were wiped out. I was back in that terrible childhood – not living, merely surviving. Even now, all this time later, I can't think of that dreadful day without tears welling in my eyes.

When it comes to my feelings about my siblings, the only possible exception is Gezzie; that's my nick-name for Gloria from the days when, as a small child, I couldn't pronounce her real name. While she and I had never been particularly close, she was horrified by the omission of my name at our mother's funeral. That said, she hadn't told me that our mother was dying or informed me when she did finally die. The first I knew about it was when I received Richard's letter.

My mother was seventy-seven when she died from a combination of septicaemia and pneumonia. I cannot erase from my mind my last sight of her. When I went to the funeral parlour the day before her burial, the lid wasn't on the coffin – I had wanted to look at her one final time. I had no feeling of trepidation or anxiety as I approached the coffin. She was in a peach dress, quite respectable, with a V-neck – but the effect was spoilt by a pair of huge glass earrings each the size of an old penny. Her fingernails were long and, as was her custom, painted blood-red. Then I noticed that in her hand she was holding a newspaper cutting. I called the assistant over and asked her to remove it so I could see what it was about. It turned out to be a story concerning my Uncle Bob, my mother's eldest brother, who'd died in a Japanese prisoner-of-war camp. It told how, as a boy, he'd gone round collecting old coats to give to poor people. I think my mother's younger sister, Teresa, must have organised the placing of the cutting in my mother's coffin.

I asked the assistant to return it to her hand and stood looking down at the face of this woman who had made my childhood such a living hell. I'd never forgotten how peaceful her own mother, Grandma Mary, had looked in her coffin, with her hands folded neatly on her chest. Not *my* mother. They say you get the face you deserve, don't they? Well, here was someone in torment. Her dyed hair was scraped back off her face, the white roots showing through at the scalp. Her skin was alabaster white, her lips an unnatural fiery red. She looked a real fright. It gives me no pleasure whatever to say this, but my mother looked exactly what she was: an ugly, wicked old witch.

And my overwhelming emotion? I was flooded with relief. My simple thought was, 'Your wickedness has gone from this earth. It's over. Thank God, it's over. You can never harm anyone else ever again.'

2

Pat and Ron

I'm not called Kim at all – and for good reason. My mother was christened Mary Patricia but, from choice, was known all her life as Pat. I was named Patricia Mary but, from as far back as I can remember, I was called Little Pat; and then, after I finally ran away from home just before my sixteenth birthday, just Pat. But I so despised that woman for what I had suffered at her hands that I decided in my twenties to rename myself Kim because my real name continued to remind me of her. I chose my new one after seeing a film starring the beautiful, blonde Kim Novak – and that's what I've been called ever since, although I've never bothered to change my name by deed poll.

My mother, Pat Shaw, was just sixteen when, at the beginning of World War II, she first met my father, Ronald McKenzie. It was in a pub, the White House, in a district of Portsmouth called Milton, just on the borders of Eastney. A Scot from

Perthshire and five years older than her, he was serving in the Royal Marines, stationed at the time at Eastney Barracks. My mother had a job at a first-aid centre in nearby Drayton.

My father was no matinee idol. He was to start losing his hair at twenty-four, and was never tall – probably no more than five foot six or seven. Both stocky and muscular, he was a strong man and fit, too – which of course he had to be as a commando. On the plus side he did have piercing blue eyes and a good sense of humour, although you wouldn't describe him as the life and soul of the party. He disapproved of women who told jokes and he hated it if any woman swore, which was a bit rich if you could have heard my mother in full flow. In many ways he was rather old-fashioned, a man of few words with a quick temper. Yet he was never violent. Not once did I see him raise a hand to my mother, and she could have brought out the devil in an archangel. Nor did he ever lay a finger on me – or if he did, I don't remember it.

But he didn't love me. I didn't realise that at first, of course, because I was too young. I had no idea what I was missing for the simple reason that I didn't know how other fathers behaved. I can honestly say, though, that I have no memory of him ever kissing me or holding me in his arms like

I saw other dads doing with their children. He was away in the war for the first three years of my life, and then he signed on for another ten years and went off to fight in Malaya. So he was an absent father at the best of times. But he never once sent me a card on my birthday or a note to say he was missing me. I was obviously out of sight, out of mind. And when he came home there were no cuddles, no feeling that he was pleased to see me. Home or away, not once in my entire childhood did he ever tell me he loved me.

Mother, by contrast to my balding, thick-set father, was gorgeous to look at. When she was fifteen, she entered a local beauty contest and came first. But the minimum age was eighteen and, when they discovered her real age, they took the title off her. Slim and tall for a woman – in heels, she looked down on my father – she had a trim frame, big bust, lovely legs and long brown hair which she made me brush for hours on end. Well-groomed, with perfectly manicured nails always painted bright red, she was undeniably a looker – and full of laughter, before the bitterness and the drink took over. She was intelligent, too, the only one of the five children in her family to win a place at grammar school.

For all that he was no oil painting, my mother fell for my father hook, line and sinker; and he couldn't resist her. Many wartime romances were superficial, a chance of fleeting happiness for two people who couldn't be sure what tomorrow would bring. Not my parents. To their dying days, I believe my father and my mother to have been the great love of each other's life. But her instability and his womanising put paid to all that.

He obviously felt a strong physical attraction to my mother from the start – but unfortunately he felt a strong physical attraction to a lot of other women too. When I was old enough to understand the expression, my Uncle Neville – my mother's youngest brother, only five years older than me and the only family member to have shown me nothing but kindness – told me my father had a reputation for being as randy as a butcher's dog. Eventually, his philandering seemed almost to unhinge my mother. There's a thin line between love and hate, and when she realised, as she did pretty early on, that he'd never abandon his womanising ways she turned into the monster she remained. Whether she'd have turned out like that anyway, I'll never know. She'd kept alive the hope that the two of them could have a future together right up to the point when she gave birth to my brother Rob, four years after me. But by then too much water had flowed under the bridge and too many bitter words had been spoken to save a relationship which I now think probably never could have been saved in the first place.

She was seven months pregnant with my elder sister, Gloria, when her first-aid centre was bombed. Portsmouth was a target throughout the war because of the docks. My parents had already married by then – you did in those days if the girl was pregnant – and were living in the house in Dunbar Road that was home to her parents, Mary and Robert, and her three younger siblings, Gordon, Teresa and Neville. My mother's eldest brother, Robert, had perished in a Japanese prisoner of war camp at the end of the war.

On 11 July 1940, while my mother was carrying a jug of water across the yard at the first-aid post, she was hit in the waist by flying shrapnel. The impact blew her and her friend, Winnie Winder, from one end of the yard to the other. I have a newspaper cutting of a piece that appeared in July 1991 in a local Portsmouth paper: my mother had been interviewed for her recollections of more than half a century earlier when the 100lb bomb fell.

Previously, each time there had been an air-raid warning my mother would cycle to her post, but never saw any action. 'On July 11,' she recalled, 'we had no reason to think anything would be different. But then we heard a thudding and gunfire and realised something was wrong.' She and Winnie ran across the yard. As they reached the door, a blast ripped through the building. Evidently, Winnie took the full force and died a few days later. My mother was badly injured by flying shrapnel. I remember as a young child seeing her stomach for the first time: the scarring extended from her waist to her crotch, like a livid mauve tree with branches coming off it. And yet, miraculously, she didn't miscarry. Gloria was obviously a strong baby because she survived the force of the blast and was born in August on Hayling Island, where my mother had temporarily moved for safety's sake. There wasn't a mark on her.

My father was back and forth, fighting in the war. On 25 March 1942, nineteen months after Gloria's arrival, I was born at Dunbar Road. Mother was nineteen. Grandma Mary later told me I'd been born with what is called a caul membrane over my face, a fine veil of skin from the amniotic sac that covers a baby's head at birth. Folklore has it that the child born with a caul will have a lucky life, which seems ironic given the household I grew up in. In the old days, sailors would pay good money for a caul and carry it with them everywhere, wrapped in cotton wool. My grandmother kept mine in a box for years, but it got lost during one of her many moves.

Although my father was only there when he was

on leave, Dunbar Road was now bursting at the seams. So, while I was still a baby, my parents, Gloria and I moved round the corner to Suffolk Road. The terraced house, like all the others in that street, must have been built in the thirties, and it's still standing today. The front door opened on to a long corridor with a room overlooking the street immediately on your right. We hardly ever used it, even though space was at a premium; it was kept for best. The corridor was covered in bright green lino, and my sister and I used to put Mansion Polish on a couple of dusters and slide up and down on them as we cleaned it for my mother. It ran to the back of the house with a staircase off to the right, leading to two bedrooms: my mother's, overlooking the road, and Gezzie's and mine, overlooking the back yard and garden.

Further down the corridor on the right there was a door into a room occupied by a lodger, Barbara, for a year or so when I was tiny. She was in the Women's Auxiliary Air Force and had somehow befriended my mother. When Barbara moved out my mother made it her own bedroom, sharing it first with my father and then with her long-time lover, James McGinley. The bedroom she'd used upstairs came in handy as she gave birth to more babies – Rob, Richard, Neil and Penny – over the next decade.

Our living room led off the end of the corridor. It contained a dresser that held all the china, a table covered with a gingham cloth and a coal fire that Gezzie and I often used to light. Then there was a scullery and a little kitchen – but no bathroom, and only an outside toilet. A big tin tub hung from a nail on a wall in the garden. Once a week, on Saturday, the tub would be brought indoors and filled with boiled water from a variety of pots and pans as each of us took our weekly bath. In the old days, it used to be the man of the house who got in first, followed by the rest all the way down to the youngest member of the family. By then, the water was so dirty you might not be able to see a little one in there; hence the expression about not throwing the baby out with the bathwater. By the time I was born, though, the tradition had changed and the youngsters went in first, the adults last.

It was a crowded house, although I could have been perfectly happy there if I'd been born into another family. But my parents seemed set against me from the start. My 'crime' was that I wasn't a boy. After one girl they'd set their hearts on a son, and I'm convinced my mother thought she could have hung on to my father if I hadn't turned out to be a girl. Throughout my childhood, my mother would often look at me and say: 'If I could send you back I would, you ugly little bitch.' My looks were my other 'crime'. I was blonde and blue-eyed, but to my mother all that meant was that I'd committed the unforgivable sin of looking just like my father, the man she loved and lost and grew to hate. I also had a similar temperament to him and some of his habits. For instance, he was never less than immaculate about his person and I've always set great store by looking the best I can. (My mother was well-groomed too, of course, but when she saw it in me she chose to associate it with her unfaithful husband.) 'You're too like your fucking father,' she'd constantly say to me. So, when she was beating me, was she giving vent to the anger she felt towards him? I can't be sure, but what I do know is that I was the only one of her children who was persistently beaten until the day I ran away from home.

If I'm a loner today – and I am – it's not too surprising. Gloria was always the favourite and she knew which side her bread was buttered. In many ways, I don't blame her for siding with our mother. In our house survival was the name of the game. Gloria was a real Artful Dodger, knowing when to speak up and when to keep quiet. She had it down to a fine art.

Throughout my childhood I longed for Gloria and me to be true sisters, united against our impossible mother. I just couldn't understand why she wouldn't stand up for me, but I now realise that not only was my sister smart enough to stay on our mother's good side, she actually got on well with her. The result was that we could never have been close. But that doesn't mean we didn't sometimes have a laugh together. Gezzie wasn't stupid. She knew the sort of carry-on that was involved for everyone trying to survive under the same roof as my mother. To a greater or lesser extent, we were all living on our nerves, which inevitably resulted in the occasional fit of the giggles.

However, Gloria had a habit of getting me into trouble. For example, our mother might ask me to go into the scullery to make her a mug of drinking chocolate. I'd mix up the powdered chocolate with some evaporated milk, and I couldn't resist spooning some of it into my mouth. Gezzie would come into the scullery after me, see that I'd used much more chocolate than was necessary, and go and tell our mother. Then, of course, I'd get a beating. I'd ask Gezzie why she told tales on me – indeed, for something she herself did if she was making a chocolate drink. But she just shrugged her shoulders.

My dream at one stage was that she and I would run away from home – which on one occasion we did, although only for a few hours – and make our way together in the world. But it was never going to happen. In the end, Gezzie's allegiance lay with my mother. It was safer for her that way. Having said that, life was much better for me if our mother wasn't around. If we were alone together, Gloria would let her guard down. But as soon as my mother returned, Gezzie would let it be known that, like her, she didn't have any time for me. My mother might say what a little bitch I was, and Gloria would immediately agree. But then, her life wouldn't have been any easier if she'd started standing up for me. Maybe she'd have started getting knocked about, too.

I can honestly say I have only a handful of happy memories from my entire childhood in connection with either of my parents, and even then they were fleeting. My earliest must have been when I was about three because the war was still on. The sirens were sounding and I remember my father giving me a piggy-back as we ran, giggling, to the Anderson air-raid shelter in our back yard. And that was it. Then he would have been gone again, back to wherever he was stationed, sometimes in the UK, sometimes abroad.

It was on one of his brief home leaves that the turning point came in his relationship with my mother. She knew his reputation for chasing after other women but didn't want to believe it, and I'm sure she felt that she could win him over with her good looks and her powers of persuasion. She was a great one for turning on the charm if she thought it might get her what she wanted – for using what she called her womanly wiles. But when it came to my father she was fighting a losing battle.

I must have been very young when he returned on this particular occasion with a gift for my mother, because I don't actually recall it – I only got told the story much later. He'd arrived home with a beautiful belt made up of different-coloured squares of leather, which he said he'd bought abroad somewhere. She was thrilled and immediately started wearing it. But a little later she found a letter that must have fallen out of one of his pockets. It was from a girl who thanked him for the belt, telling him she would always treasure it and saying how much she was looking forward to seeing him again. My mother was wearing the belt as she read this letter.

It was the final straw, and it broke my mother's heart. In many ways she was never the same again, because she now knew once and for all that she could never trust him around other women. Grandma Mary once told me that my father's mother had been so relieved when her son had joined the Royal Marines because she thought it would be the making of him. My father had been a real tearaway up in Perth – no girl was safe with him, she'd said, because he was so oversexed. Many years later, my mother implied that she and my father had had a good sex life. So I don't think she could understand why he'd bothered to have dalliances with other women. It must have made her feel inadequate – and she minded, of course, because she loved him.

Up until the time of the incident with the belt, I have hazy memories of her running a good house. But I have no recollection of her ever being a loving mother. She never showed me any affection, never once cuddled me or sat me on her lap or tucked me into bed at night and read me a story. I can dimly remember her at the stove, though, cooking egg and bacon or a nice roast dinner. But the country was in the grip of rationing, so there wasn't much to go round. Towards the end of the week, as the money ran short, it would be spam sandwiches. A treat would be a Mars bar – a whole week's sweet ration – sliced up so everyone had a piece. Afterwards, she'd sit knitting cardigans for us with rabbits down the front or work at her Singer sewing machine, making little gingham dresses for Gezzie and me. But those days didn't last long.

As my mother got eaten up with bitterness and turned increasingly to alcohol, so she became more and more abusive and neglectful. But it takes a small child some time to work out that not all mothers behave like this. Later on, when I went to the local school, I'd see mums picking up their daughters at the end of the day and bending down and kissing them. 'Shall we go and get an ice cream, love?' they'd say and off they'd trot, mother and daughter, hand-in-hand. I'd watch these everyday incidents and be overwhelmed by a sense of sadness. I never knew what it was like to hold my mother's hand. In fact, the only way I knew what her hand felt like was when she used it to slap me round the face.

My earliest memory of serious violence is in Suffolk Road when I was four and my father was home on leave. My mother had been drinking and a row had begun – probably over his womanising. Whatever the reason, I became the innocent victim caught in the crossfire. I was beaten so badly that my mother marched me down to a big building where we were led into a room with painted yellow tiles on the walls. She wanted to show my injuries to an NSPCC officer. In my mind's eye I can still see lovely Inspector Weeks, with his full head of white hair and kind voice. He told me to stand next to a bed that folded down from the wall but was attached to it by chains. The side of the bed came up to my chest. I was facing Inspector Weeks when he asked me to take off my top. Then, in a gentle voice, he said: 'Turn round, love.' I did as I was told. To this day, I can hear the sharp intake of breath as he caught sight of my back. From neck to waist I was covered in bruises, black, yellow and blue. And there were marks, too, all down the side of my body where I'd been repeatedly punched.

My mother sat there with a satisfied smile on her face. She couldn't have cared less about my suffering – her only motivation in taking me to the authorities had been a desire for revenge. 'Look at what my husband has done to our little girl,' she must have told the inspector, determined to get my father into as much trouble as she knew how. As I've grown older, it's occurred to me that it could have been my mother who assaulted me and not my father. She could have been the one who, in her drunken anger, had lashed out at me and then placed the blame squarely at my father's door. Many years later, he told me my mother had once tried to get him into trouble for beating me when it was in fact her doing. Certainly, it's true that she beat me repeatedly throughout my childhood with anything that came to hand: clothes brushes, wooden coathangers, brooms. But I'll never know for sure which of my parents turned my body black and blue before I was taken to the NSPCC. In any case, nothing came of this incident. Inspector Weeks visited the house a few times and then my mother was left to her own devices. There was much less supervision in those days.

The arguments in our house weren't normal, healthy ones – you couldn't do right for doing wrong. Anything could set my mother off and it was ten times worse if she'd been drinking. She'd eff and blind and run out of the front door into the road in her undies, screaming the place down at any time of day or night. Her favourite tipple was VP port wine. In time, I'd be sent to the off-licence to buy it for her. She liked it because it was strong – well, you could have bleached the toilet with it – so it meant she could get drunk quicker. My Uncle Gordon, the next brother down from her, once told me she was already a drinker as a teenager. She'd come reeling home at sixteen, he remembers, unable to stand up straight. And it was quite unusual in those days for a woman, never mind a young girl, to be a heavy drinker. Sometimes we couldn't afford to eat, but she was never without her drink or her cigarettes – she was a chain-smoker all her life.

Periods of calm were rare, days when everything was quiet and ordered few and far between. If I'd been playing in the street, I'd dread coming back indoors because I never knew what I'd be walking into. If my mother was in one of her moods, she'd hit me just because she felt like it. I remember tiptoeing past her in the kitchen on one occasion as she hung over the heavy oven door, threatening to end it all. (The gas was never switched on at such moments, of course.) As I passed her, she kicked me for no reason.

'You wouldn't care if I killed myself, would you, you little cow?' she shouted.

I ran into the garden and sent up a silent prayer. 'Please God,' I said, 'please let her die.'

And the joke was that she always had such a high opinion of herself. She'd have spent half the night screaming blue murder, indoors and out, with the police on the doorstep yet again. Then she'd be out the next morning, walking up the street swinging her arms as though she were Queen of the May and looking down her nose at the neighbours. But Gezzie and I would see them laughing at her behind her back. Our road was poor but respectable. The husbands were away at war and the wives were doing their best to cope, day by day. They were hardworking and they loved their kids. To them, our mother was a vile, drunken, debauched creature and it spilled over on to us. We were treated like lepers by other children who would have heard their parents talk about us – and not because of how *we* behaved but because of how *she* did. I don't know if the neighbours knew about the beatings, although the house walls were so thin they must have heard something. I never remember anyone knocking at the front door to see if everything was all right, though. I think the general attitude must have been that this was a bad house, one to be avoided at all costs. I don't blame them. The police were at our door almost every night and no neighbour wanted to get caught up in that.

In the circumstances – I had no one looking out for me; Gloria would side with my mother; my father was away and, anyway, I wasn't the son he'd longed for – I was unhappy and lonely all the time. It's curious, then, that my Uncle Neville remembers me as a happy-go-lucky kid. I always had a big smile on my face, he says; and it's true. I got it into my head early on that I wouldn't let anyone know my true feelings, so I wore a more or less permanent smile like a mask. I was embarrassed by my unhappiness.

I wasn't a child to invent imaginary friends, but I do remember I had a kewpie doll I'd play with on my own in the bedroom I shared with Gezzie. At Christmas, she and I would make decorations out of brightly coloured crepe paper. We'd cut it into circles and stitch them together to make balls which we'd then hang from the ceiling. When Christmas was over I gathered up these crepe paper balls, cut a hole in the centre and then put them over the head of my kewpie doll so that she had a collection of about fifteen different 'dresses'. I'd play with her for hours, but didn't dare bring her or her extensive wardrobe downstairs for fear that, in one of her tempers, my mother would throw the lot on the fire. There was no television in those days and we didn't have a telephone; but we did listen to the radio. I remember all of us listening to *Dick Barton, Special Agent* in the scullery, and my mother making me brush her hair for what seemed like hours on end. But really I preferred being on my own, because that way I was less likely to suffer on account of my mother's terrible mood swings. I'd go up to the bedroom and read my *Girl's Crystal* comic or dream of one day being a Hollywood film star. Even then I knew I had something of the performer in me – I found the idea of standing up in front of an audience quite appealing.

Now, as I look back, I see my mother as a woman full of anger and hatred and cruelty. Was she perhaps mentally disturbed? I'll never know. But I now realise she was like her father, who was a bad-tempered man with a cruel streak. Certainly she was her father's favourite child – not surprisingly, since they had such similar personalities.

My mother's mother, Grandma Mary, also had a temper but she'd had a hard life. She was a decent woman and a loyal wife who never looked at another man even after her husband left her. Born and raised in Ireland, she'd been taken into a convent in Co. Cork as a novice. But she never got to take her vows. I don't know the reason, but apparently Grandma got so angry one day that she broke a slate – the sort children wrote on in the classroom in the old days – over Mother Superior's head. Grandma was banished from the convent on the spot.

After her husband walked out – to go and live with a woman by whom, unknown to Grandma, he already had two kids – he gave her no money and wouldn't sign over the lease of Dunbar Road into her name. That meant Grandma was living hand-to-mouth and always looking for a roof to put over the head of herself and her youngest child, my Uncle Neville, whom she was left to raise single-handedly. To begin with, they came to live in Suffolk Road with my mother, Gloria and me. But my mother was always picking fights with her for no reason, and then Grandma would be thrown out and have to find a bedsit for herself and Neville. She'd put a piece of string down the middle of the room and hang a blanket over it to give each of them some privacy during the night. Uncle Neville tells me that it was always Grandma who was the peacemaker after one of these bust-ups with my mother, but it must have been very hard at times. I clearly remember Grandma saying to my mother, 'You're not mad, just plain evil.' My guess is that she was probably both, in equal measure.

3

The Other Man

My mother first met James McGinley – in fact everyone called him Mac – before I was born. He was already a firm friend of my father's. The same age, they'd first met when both had signed up with the Marines in 1936. Mac was from Sunderland where he and his brother, John, had been raised in a dirt-poor but loving environment; their father had lost an arm in World War I.

In time, both my father and Mac were stationed in Portsmouth and it wasn't long before Mac was brought back to Dunbar Road. My mother, I was later told, was six months pregnant with me at the time, so it must have been December 1941. Physically, beyond the fact that both had fair hair and blue eyes the two men were totally unalike. Mac was a six-footer, slim and with not an ounce of surplus flesh on him but with a muscular chest and back. He was a quiet, gentle man, but I'd have to say a weak one, too, although full of fun. I had cause to suffer at his hands throughout my childhood and yet my lasting memory of Mac is that essentially he was a good man. His misfortune was to meet a bully of a woman.

There was obviously an attraction between my mother and Mac, but I've always believed that she started an affair with him mainly as a way of making my father jealous and getting him to commit to her. She wanted my father to stop his two-timing ways but, much as he loved my mother, he was the sort of man who always needed women on the side. At first my father had no idea that my mother was having an affair with Mac, but bit by bit it became apparent; and nor did she care – she wanted to provoke him. My father was a proud man, though. It was one thing for him to carry on with a succession of women; quite another for his wife to be sleeping with his best friend. I'm told there were fisticuffs. But Mac could look after himself. For years afterwards, he'd laugh and joke and tell anyone who'd listen, 'Ron was so much shorter than me, I couldn't catch the little bugger!'

There must have been a period when my mother was sleeping with both my father and Mac. She had another pregnancy after me that went to full term and produced a girl, Rose, who was born with a crippled spine and only lived for a matter of days. My mother always swore that the baby was my father's although I don't see how she could have been absolutely sure, even if she thought she was telling the truth. In time, and as it became increasingly clear that my father was never going to return to the fold, she and Mac began to live together openly. Mac would make himself scarce, of course, whenever my father came home on leave, but after he was posted to Malaya these occasions became much rarer.

My earliest memories of Mac are of him standing by the mantelpiece in the living room in Suffolk Road sharpening his cut-throat razor before having a shave. I can also picture him polishing the brass buttons on his uniform, so he must still have been in the Marines. But whereas my father signed on for a further ten years after he'd completed his original twelve, Mac didn't want to carry on. Grandma Mary used to say of my father, 'If that man had cared about you kids, he would never have signed on for extra service.' And she had a point. Eventually my mother told me that I had to call Mac 'Dad'. I liked him well enough but he wasn't my father, so he always remained Mac to me. That sort of thing has to come naturally – you can't force it.

While my father was still around my parents played cat and mouse with each other, and Gezzie and I were always caught in the middle as they fought and broke up and got back together and then started fighting all over again. But in the end my mother came to accept that she'd never make a go of the marriage. So when Gloria was three or four and I wasn't much more than a toddler, she took off with Mac. To this day, I'm not sure why. They found rooms in Albert Road in Portsmouth, or so I've been told, while they lived on Mac's meagre pension from the Marines as he looked in vain for a permanent job. Then again, maybe they wanted to be together without the threat of my father turning up. Or maybe she was simply fed up with having to look after two small children. I'll never know the full story. And my father was off fighting, so *he* couldn't look after us – not that my mother was concerned one way or the other.

When Mac and my mother first took off, at my father's suggestion Grandma and her youngest son, my Uncle Neville, who couldn't have been more than seven at the time, moved into Suffolk Road to look after Gezzie and me. My father offered to pay the rent because he didn't want to lose the house and Grandma was only too willing to be there because it meant that for once she was being offered the opportunity of living somewhere halfway decent – and, what's more, rent-free. For the first time in a long time, she and Nev could afford to eat properly. But Grandma found it hard to cope. Nev, being older than us girls, went to school every day, but she had various cleaning jobs which took her out of the house and meant she found it hard also to look after Gezzie and me. That's when we were placed in our first foster home.

My sister and I would spend a few weeks in one and then be collected again without warning by our mother. A month or so later, and again without warning we'd be dumped in another. The two things a child wants in life are unconditional love and security. I had neither. Such home life as we had may have been cold and brutal – but better the devil you know. When that permanence was denied me, my life disintegrated into turmoil.

Many years later Grandma told me she had come to visit Gloria and me in one foster home and had been horrified. Conditions were spartan, to say the least. But what shocked her most – and she would refer to this time and again – was that, when she looked into my cot, it was jumping with fleas. Why couldn't Grandma take us back to Suffolk Road, we used to wonder. But of course she couldn't possibly have coped with three kids under ten as well as having to work unsocial hours.

I can't actually remember any of the foster homes, but among my earliest memories – I can't have yet been four – is the time when Gezzie and I were placed in somewhere called the Services House on the seafront at Southsea. I think it's now no longer a children's home but one for old people. At that stage, Mac and my mother had moved up to London out of my father's reach as they looked for work. My father enjoyed making their life as difficult as possible if they were living anywhere in Portsmouth. If he was back on leave or stationed nearby, he'd find out their new address and then go and tell the landlady that they weren't married. In those days, that was considered very sinful, so they'd immediately be thrown out. Throughout this whole chaotic period, though, and whether Gezzie and I were with foster families or in children's homes, my mother never once came to visit us.

By the time I was left in the Services House I was feeling very confused and alone, and I can remember how much I used to cry. But although I didn't want to be there, there were some compensations. There was a big toy room and an enclosed yard with swings where we could play. The food was good, served in a huge dining room with glass walls like a conservatory. I was introduced to dishes like spotted dick and bread and butter pudding. And the staff were kind. But I was also wetting the bed every night. Gloria and I slept in the same bed and I used to tell the people who worked there that she'd been the one who'd wet the sheets. I can still recall my embarrassment.

The Services House was for children whose fathers were away fighting or who'd died, and whose mothers couldn't cope or had run off. You would stay there until your family situation improved or you were fostered or adopted. After about six months, though, the authorities must have woken up to the fact that Gezzie and I had two perfectly able-bodied parents. Yes, my father was in the Marines but there was no reason why my mother couldn't look after their two little girls. We were taking up much-needed space. So our parents were told that we had to leave.

That's when my father did a deal with my mother. She could live in Suffolk Road, he said, with or without Mac, if she paid the rent. In return, she had to reclaim Gloria and me from the Services House. And since she had to live somewhere she agreed to his offer, however reluctantly – she hated losing any battle with my father. So we were back at home permanently – or so I supposed. But nothing ever lasted long in my life.

I was four when Robert was born in July 1946. While she was pregnant, my mother tried to tell my father that it was his baby. And when it turned out to be a much-prized boy she kept up the pretence – although, who knows, she may have genuinely believed it herself, as my father would still come and visit if he was back on leave and Mac was out at work. I'll never know the truth of that situation. I remember my first sight of Rob. Gezzie and I were sitting in the living room when Mac and the doctor came out of the downstairs room where Barbara had once lodged and where my mother had just given birth. Dr Powell handed Robert to Mac and he came towards us. 'Here's your brother,' he said, beaming with pride.

Gradually, it became obvious that Robert must be Mac's son. The boy was blond, like both men, but slim rather than stocky. As a result, Rob was the only child apart from me who'd get on the wrong side of my mother. I was belted partly because I reminded my mother of my father. Rob grew to look just like Mac, so if she'd had another of her many fallings-out with him she might decide to take it out on Rob for no better reason than that he reminded her of Mac. It didn't take much to start her off. But whereas Rob might get the occasional slap, I'd really be beaten – not every now and then but once, twice, three times a week. In the end she had nine surviving children; I was the only one who was abused on a regular basis.

For years, while there'd been some doubt, my mother nursed the belief that, if Robert was felt to be Ron's child, he just might come back for good.

But it was never going to happen. My father was an intensely proud man and a private one, too. He'd seen the sort of person my mother had become, and wasn't prepared to be embarrassed by her. Nothing would have made him live in the same house as a woman whose behaviour was the talk of Portsmouth – he'd heard the tales of drunken brawling in the street with my mother screaming abuse at Mac half the night. In a way I can understand why he signed on for another ten years in the Marines, but as a child I felt let down by him and angry, too. He was off round the world and he obviously preferred that to being with us. I used to make excuses to myself about why he saw so little of us, and to pray that he'd come and rescue me from my misery. But gradually I came to realise he couldn't give a damn about Gloria or me. Even so, I'd have given anything to live with him, because then, I thought, there'd be no more abuse, no more beatings.

But I was stuck in Suffolk Road, whether I liked it or not; and the bad atmosphere was getting worse. Mac had found life very hard after he was demobbed. He'd been a teenager when he signed on, and in the Marines they didn't teach you any skills beyond fighting. Back in Civvy Street, he didn't have much to offer: he searched and searched, but just couldn't find work. Finally, he got a job locally at a place called the Flexible Packaging Company, which manufactured plastic bags for food storage. He certainly was one of the world's workers. He'd be up early in the morning to make his own docker's butties, as they were known – great big doorstep sandwiches filled with dripping and corned beef or spam – and a flask of tea, and then off he'd go on his bike. He never failed to bring his wages home. My mother didn't know how fortunate she was. But then she was good at getting everyone, including us little children, to pull their weight as she sat around smoking and drinking.

As soon as Rob was born, Gezzie and I were expected to look after his basic needs as well as doing other heavy chores around the house. We had to scrape the baby's nappies after he'd filled them. We used toilet paper, which we then had to take to the outside toilet and flush away. To get the nappies clean – there were no such things as disposables in those days – we had to scrub them with a bar of green Fairy soap and then drop them into something called the copper, in fact a big aluminium pan in which water was boiled over a gas flame. It got the washing cleaner than anything we've got today. The two of us were also responsible for emptying the water after everyone had had their weekly bath in the tub we brought in from the garden. We'd use pans until the water level was reduced to only a few inches, then drag the bathtub across the floor and into the garden where we'd tip it over. We had to strip our own beds, too, and wash the sheets. By the time I was six I had to iron them as well.

It was wrong to make young children do work like that, although I have to admit that even at such an early age I took to cleaning. I must have inherited it from Grandma Mary, who liked everything spotless. I've always found it very satisfying to take something dirty and make it clean – I can't bear a mark on anything. For instance, in our road the woman of the house would swill the step outside the front door with warm, soapy water each morning, then go over the step and pathway with a stiff broom and finally sweep the water out onto the pavement where it met the water swept out there by each of her neighbours. That way, the whole street was kept clean. As my mother wasn't often out of her bed until mid-morning, it was a task that fell to Gloria or me before we went off to school. With my passion for cleaning I quite liked it, but the neighbours would look disapprovingly at me down on my knees. Once again, my mother had made herself look heartless in their eyes.

Not, of course, that she cared about their opinions, much less apologised for the noisy, disruptive rows she started. For instance, she was the one who got Mac fired from the Flexible Packaging Company. The pattern was always the same. They'd have one row too many and either she'd throw him out or he'd leave home of his own accord for a while. He wasn't a promiscuous man, so I don't believe he was with another woman on these occasions. I think he'd just take a room somewhere or stay with a mate from work to get a bit of peace and quiet. A typical row would flare up over the smallest thing and it was always, always initiated by my mother. Mac might arrive home at the end of the working day and she'd accuse him of being five minutes late. He'd probably had to cycle home in heavy traffic – and anyway, what did five minutes matter? But she wouldn't leave it alone. This was a woman who just loved trouble. An hour later and they'd be knocking each other round the house, the row having escalated into a pitched battle. At this point she'd kick him out of the house, and he might be gone for two or three days.

Then my mother would get bored. She'd send Gezzie and me up to the factory and ask to see Mac – with a bit of blackmail thrown in for good measure. The man on the gate got to know us well. 'Oh, you kids again,' he'd say. 'I'll go and get him.' As soon as Mac appeared we'd have to tell him that, if he didn't come home immediately, we wouldn't be allowed inside – or she'd put Rob in the garden wearing just a vest, and that's where he'd stay until Mac got home. And this could be the middle of winter.

What choice did he have? But it couldn't carry on. My mother sent us up there once too often, made one too many nuisance phone calls. One day his boss said, 'Look, Mac, you're a lovely man, but unless you can get your private life sorted out, we can't keep you on. It's too disruptive.' So he got the sack. When Mac got back home he sat down and sobbed his heart out, then turned to my mother and said, 'You've lost me my job.'

She was totally unrepentant. 'Well, you shouldn't have walked out, should you?' she retorted, looking at him as though he were a piece of filth.

Other men would have left for good long before. But Mac was a passive man and, anyway, he simply couldn't afford to. His pay packet went on raising his increasing brood of children. He'd never have let them down financially, and there would have been very little left over for himself if he'd gone to live on his own. But actually he didn't want that. He wanted to be with my mother – if only she would calm down and let everyone lead a peaceful life. As it happened, losing his job at the packaging company wasn't the end of the world. Not too long afterwards he was taken on at Southampton Docks painting liners. Despite having no formal training, he was good at it. But it meant cycling from Portsmouth to Southampton and back every day, a round trip of forty miles.

At heart, Mac was a good man. My Uncle Neville always got on well with him. Nev didn't like my father, though. He tells a story from the time when my father was still living in Suffolk Road and Grandma Mary and Neville were there, too. Nev was mad keen on football and always read the newspaper starting from the back, to get all the latest sports news. My father would pick up the paper first but when he'd finished he wouldn't hand it over to Nev. He'd stand up, put it under the cushion on his chair, and then sit down again so that Nev couldn't get it. Can you imagine anything so childish? What a petty, spiteful way for a grown man to behave towards a young boy.

Mac too was quite keen on football. Nev will never forget, he says, the first time he laid eyes on him. By the age of ten he was playing for his school team, and a lot of people used to come and watch the games. On one occasion my mother turned up with a man Nev had never seen before. It turned out to be Mac, so she'd obviously gone public with their relationship by then. I think Nev came to regard him as a surrogate father or favourite uncle. They'd go to football matches together and then, when Nev was older, meet in a pub for a beer or two. In fact, Nev got closer to Mac than he'd ever been to my mother, his own sister. He preferred to stay at the house of his friend, Geoff, just a few doors up on Suffolk Road, than to be at my mother's. She never made him feel welcome, he said.

A year after Robert arrived, Richard was born. In 2000, when she was dying, my mother apparently told Gloria in a mocking tone that Mac wasn't Richard's father; she claimed that Ron was. I'm convinced that was just her getting her final revenge. Whatever the truth, when Richard was three months old Mac took him up to his parents in Sunderland. It was meant to be a temporary solution while Mac looked for work down south; but Mac and my mother never did fetch Richard home throughout his childhood. Crazy as this may sound, in drink my mother would taunt Mac about Richard. 'You promised you'd go and get your son,' she'd say. 'But you never have. What sort of a father does that make you?' Yes, and what sort of a mother did that make her?

But it was worse than that. After Mac had left Richard with his parents, my mother not only said nothing to the authorities about his whereabouts but continued to claim family allowance for him as though she was raising him in Suffolk Road. Mac's mother – Richard's grandmother – had little or no money to start with and now she had another mouth to feed. She wrote to my mother time and again, asking her to tell the authorities the situation so that she could legitimately claim the allowance up in Sunderland. But my mother completely ignored her letters and went on drawing an allowance for Richard in Portsmouth.

Mac's mother was reluctant to 'shop' my mother – I don't think she wanted to get her son into trouble by association – but in the end she had no choice. After two years she finally wrote to Social Services and my mother was taken to court. Care for the baby was officially made over to his grandmother, who was then entitled to receive eight shillings a week family allowance – 40p in today's money, worth more then than it is now but still not a lot. Nevertheless, it helped her a little. My mother was also ordered to hand over to Richard's grandmother two years' back payment of family allowance, but she never did so. She simply said she hadn't got the money, and no one ever tried to enforce the judgement.

Meanwhile, the screaming rows continued and Mac was regularly thrown out of the house. If he couldn't find a bed at a friend's he sometimes ended up in the shelter in nearby Bransbury Park, and Gezzie and I would track him down there. He'd be cold and bedraggled and hungry, but he'd still come back to the house for yet more humiliation. One of her favourite tricks was to order him to beg for forgiveness. 'On your knees, you grovelling bastard!' she'd snarl. And he'd always have to do it, what's more, in front of Gloria and me. Only then was he allowed to stand up. I hated it. It was so sad to see a man behaving like that – and over an argument he hadn't even begun. If a row flared up after Gezzie and I had gone to bed, she'd yell up the stairs that she wanted us down with her right away. We'd have to sit there as she hurled insults at him. 'You're not a fucking man!' she'd scream. 'You're a fucking pig. You came from a slum in Sunderland. Your filthy, fucking parents . . .' And that would always do it. He'd erupt in fury and grab her, hitting her wherever he could land a punch. In all honesty I couldn't blame him, because she'd goaded him until he could take no more. These fights exploded all around me, week in, week out, throughout my childhood. I know Gloria didn't like it either, but she seemed to weather it better than I did – I was living on my nerves all the time.

Early in her relationship with Mac my mother had gone with him to a railway station because he said he was going back to Sunderland to see his parents. But as she was walking away she looked back and saw him crossing to another platform and boarding a different train. When he got home, she screamed the place down and forced him to admit he'd been to see a girl called Greta; my mother said he'd fallen in love with her, which he denied. And she wouldn't let it go. Down the years, if she'd been drinking and she remembered Greta, she'd taunt him about her. 'You were in love with that whore,' she'd insist, 'the one with syphilis. So what does that make you, you dirty bastard?' And she'd be shouting this in front of Gezzie and me, two little girls who shouldn't have known about such things.

She and Mac were fond of going to the dogs, but of course she'd drink heavily at the racetrack. This was fine if she won, because she'd be in a good mood for as long as her winnings lasted. But if she lost, that meant trouble. She'd start picking a fight with Mac as though it was his fault her dog hadn't raced home first. I'd be lying in bed and suddenly become aware of her voice, screeching and swearing as she staggered back down Suffolk Road. That's when I knew I was in for a bad night. She'd roll in through the front door calling Mac every name under the sun, and before long she'd call up the stairwell for Gezzie and me to get out of our beds and come and witness yet another vicious assault.

She'd hit and kick him until he could take no more. Then he'd head for the door and she'd go screaming after him. I could see all the lights coming on in the neighbouring houses, knowing I'd be in school next day – if I escaped being beaten so badly that I couldn't go – sitting beside kids who'd heard all this uproar in the middle of the night. I'd pray that the drink would get to her and she'd fall into a semi-conscious sleep. But it took an awful lot to put her out. Sometimes I'd get hit, too; sometimes not. There was no pattern, just the irrational actions of a vicious, heartless woman.

Most weeks the neighbours would end up calling the police when she started running up and down the street screaming obscenities, with Mac going after her and trying to pull her back indoors. And yet, in all the years the police turned up on the doorstep, she said she wanted to press charges on only one occasion. Mac was forced to spend the night in a police cell, and was subsequently fined. That meant, of course, that he had a police record, something my mother used as ammunition. Ever afterwards, if he'd taken so much violence from her that he went to retaliate, she'd immediately threaten him: 'Hit me back and I'll call the police!' And she'd continue to call him every name under the sun. They both knew he'd be likely to go to prison for a second offence. What a position of power she was in, and how she loved it! None the less he would occasionally hit her back – but she was canny enough not to report him. He would be no use to her if he was serving a prison sentence. She enjoyed blackmailing him, but at the end of the day she wanted the money he brought into the house.

Mac should have stood up to her, of course. Yet I couldn't bring myself to hate him, even though I suffered enough beatings at his hands – always egged on by my mother. But he was much more reliable and loving than my father. In many ways he was a gentle, cultured man. He'd listen to classical music, or he'd get out his paintbrush if anywhere in the house had started looking shabby. He made himself responsible for the upkeep of the garden, which he enjoyed – but then he'd been blessed with green fingers. And he bought some rabbits for Gezzie and me. They were kept in a hutch under the lilac tree and I used to play with them for hours. Such nice times as I remember from my childhood were always with Mac. I think he must have been posted to Egypt during World War II because, if he came back from the pub in a happy frame of mind, he'd sometimes wrap himself in a sheet, put a fez on his head and then sing a funny little song with Arabic-sounding words. It would make Gezzie and me howl with laughter.

But happy times were few and far between

because my mother was so totally unpredictable. You might ask her an innocent question like whether she wanted anything from the shops, and she'd just wheel round and slap you across the face. 'If I want something from the shops, I'll fucking ask you for it!' One of my worst beatings was the result of a misunderstanding about shopping. I'd been sent up the road to get a few bits and pieces. When I got back, she was in the scullery having another stand-up row with Mac. I could see she was in a filthy temper. She grabbed the shopping from me and then demanded why I hadn't bought her any cigarettes. I told her I hadn't known I was meant to. She turned to Mac. Had he asked me to buy cigarettes for her? He said he couldn't remember. Maybe he had, maybe he hadn't. 'Don't stand up for her!' she screeched. 'I know I asked her to fucking buy them. So if I give her a good hiding she'll remember in future, won't she?' And Mac just stood there as she dragged me up the corridor into the front room and beat the living daylights out of me across my back and bum with a wooden coathanger. The pain was excruciating. When she decided I'd been punished enough, she threw the hanger on the floor and walked out of the room. I waited till she'd gone and then ran up to my bedroom, curled myself into a little ball on my bed and cried my eyes out. No one came to comfort me – not my sister, and Mac wouldn't have dared.

If she was feeling particularly vicious she'd reach for the most painful weapon, the carpet brush, and hit me repeatedly on the elbow. One day she asked me to go to the shops for a few things and put a ten shilling note (50p) on the table to pay for them. I went up to my bedroom to brush my hair and get my coat, and five minutes later she came screaming up the stairs. 'I said go now, not when you fucking feel like it!' And with that I was dragged downstairs and given a carpet brush beating on my elbow. Her behaviour was, as ever, totally irrational, and it meant that everybody else was on edge all the time.

It's perfectly clear that all Mac wanted was a quiet life, but that was never going to be possible with my mother. Hard as it is to accept, I think he must have been genuinely fond of her. He used to call her Angel. One February, when we were still in Suffolk Road, he went to the local Co-op in Eastney and brought home a cake for her birthday. The message piped on the icing was: 'To my Angel, for her birthday'. Gezzie and I were giggling behind our hands. 'Some bloody angel,' my sister whispered. I can't remember the reason for my mother's temper that day – there didn't have to be one – but she picked up the cake, took one look at it and hurled it against the wall.

Mac just sighed and went into the garden. He had to stay for the children's sake, and I know he cared for them. After Robert, Richard and Neil, Mac and my mother eventually went on to have four girls: Penny, Rosemary, Caroline and Janet. So, for all their tempestuous rows, they had seven children together – although they were spread out over many years. I'd left home before the younger two girls were born. Even so, Mac and my mother never married. She'd go on and on about it. 'You've given me all these bastards,' she'd shout. 'The least you can do is make an honest woman of me.' But he never did. And can you blame him?

In any normal family, the arrival of a new baby is cause for celebration. But my mother wasn't remotely maternal, and I often wondered why she and Mac didn't practise some sort of birth control. Her life was chaotic, though, and fuelled by alcohol so, as with everything else, she must have viewed sex as something to be enjoyed when the fancy took her – and if it resulted in another baby, well, so be it. Certainly, her pregnancies didn't affect my mother's drinking: she just carried on as before.

As a result of her attitude to motherhood, her children weren't close to each other. We simply didn't operate like other families. Each one of us was living in his or her own little world. Rob would run around outside with his mates. Gezzie got on quite well with him, but I preferred Neil. I was eight when he was born and he was a sweet little boy. By and large, though, in our household a new baby meant only one thing: more work for Gloria and me. If one of the babies woke up in the night and cried, it was Gezzie or I who would have to get up to see to them. My mother never stirred – but then she was always sleeping off the effects of too much alcohol.

I shan't easily forget the final days of her pregnancy with Neil. She and Mac were in the middle of another row. It was mid-morning so he must have been laid off from painting the liners, something that happened every so often. He and my mother were in the downstairs bedroom screaming at each other when the doorbell rang. I went to open it, to find my father standing on the step in full military uniform. He barely acknowledged either Gloria or me, and said he wanted a word with Mac and our mother.

Mac appeared in the corridor and asked what the hell Ron was doing there. My father said he was fed up with having to pay part of his Admiralty allowance for Rob, since it had been clear to him for a couple of years at least that he was Mac's son. At that moment my mother, eight months pregnant, appeared from the bedroom without a stitch on. My father took one look at her. 'For Christ's sake, Pat,' he said, 'get some clothes on.' But she just stood her ground. I think she'd already started on the VP wine. Whether she thought the sight of her would turn him on, I don't know.

After a while, though, she did put on a dressing gown and then my father went into the bedroom with her and Mac and repeated the reason for his visit. My mother wouldn't hear of it. 'You signed a fucking form to keep him,' she insisted. 'Your name's on the fucking birth certificate as his father. There's nothing you can fucking do about it.' Gezzie and I were sitting on the stairs eavesdropping. Yet again, our mother, our drunken, foul-mouthed, abusive mother, had won a battle with our father while keeping her lover coming back for more.

4

The Nuns of Nazareth House

My mother may have enjoyed her temporary moment of triumph in getting my father to continue to help pay for Robert's upkeep. But he wasn't going to let it rest there. Neither of them was ever worried about using us as pawns in their power games, which almost always involved money. Now that my father had come to the realisation that Robert wasn't his child, he was determined to reduce by a third the Admiralty allowance to which he was entitled for Gezzie, Robert and me and which he handed over to my mother. Her response was to tell him that, if she didn't receive regular money for us three kids, she wouldn't keep any of us. There was a massive dispute, he called her bluff, it didn't work and she dumped us in a place called Nazareth House.

Gezzie was seven and I was six. In most of the homes we'd been placed in previously I'd been lonely and bewildered, but no one had been actively cruel to me. For as long as I live, I will never, ever forget the cruelty of the nuns who ran the Nazareth House establishments. They were Catholic convents, and there were a number of them all over the country. The first one where Gezzie, Robert and I were placed was in Romsey in Hampshire. Rob wasn't with us for long, though, because my father did a deal with Grandma Mary. He said that she and Neville could come back and live in Suffolk Road if she'd also look after the three children. This sort of bargain had been struck before, of course: after leaving Dunbar Road, Grandma Mary and Nev lived in a successsion of bedsits or in Suffolk Road, depending on how well she was getting on with Mother. But she maintained – realistically, I'm sure – that she could only manage Rob. So he was rescued from Nazareth House and Gloria and I were left on our own. My mother and Mac, meanwhile, or so Nev told me years later, had decided to move to London to try their luck there.

The nuns told us they were the wives of Jesus, and I always believed he was a good man. What I couldn't understand, in that case, was why his 'wives' could behave in such a heartless way in his name. These were cowardly women who I can only imagine couldn't cope with the outside world. In the convent, all their needs were catered for. And yet, they seemed incapable of showing any kindness to all these little girls living away from home. Instead of offering a warm and loving atmosphere, Nazareth House seemed full of fear to a six-year-old child. But this time it wasn't just me who was picked on; the nuns were vile to all of us.

The building at Romsey was dark and cloistered, and had a chapel within its walls. The sisters wore long, dark robes to the ground, their hair totally covered beneath hooded cowls; the younger nuns, the novices, were dressed in white. All of them prayed morning, noon and night, and we had to do the same until we were dropping with tiredness. During the six months that Gezzie and I were there, one of the older nuns died. But they didn't place her body in a coffin. They put it on the altar in the chapel and made us walk up to view it, so close you could have touched her. And then we had to pray for her soul. I was terrified and couldn't get the image of her waxen face out of my mind. I don't think any of us children had ever seen a dead person before, and yet no one showed us any sympathy or made it something we could properly understand. Most of us were crying with fear. In my opinion, the sisters should never have involved us in her death in the first place.

The nuns were also teaching us and they were unbelievably, unnecessarily strict. On each of their desks was a large twig that had been cut from a tree and all the knots and whorls left on it. If one of us got an answer wrong or didn't know it or were a little slow in speaking up the sister who was taking that lesson would grab the twig, tell us to place our outspread hand on the desk and then hit it as hard as she could. The sharp bits of the wood would cut into our flesh and sometimes make it bleed. It really hurt, and we weren't meant to make any noise when we were hit.

Gloria, with her bright red hair, always had a rebellious streak and I have to admire her for it. On one occasion one of the nuns, Sister Ignatius, told her to perform a task and she refused. 'Right, put your hand out,' she was told. But she wouldn't. 'Hit me,' said Gezzie, 'and I'll hit you back!' And, with that she picked up the twig, hit Sister Ignatius round her head and stormed out of the classroom. Of course, she was sent to bed with nothing to eat. Gezzie didn't care, though. She may only have been seven at the time but she had spirit.

It was a desperately unhappy time. We were either working or praying, and there was no respite at weekends when we were taken in a crocodile on mile-long walks, in all weathers, led by one sister and with another at the back of the snaking line of small girls. We were forbidden to talk and were often freezing as we were only dressed in little jackets and skirts and had no more than socks to cover our legs, while the sisters stayed nice and warm in their flowing robes. There was also a tradition that one of the sisters would appear on a Saturday with a contraption like a cinema usherette's tray of ice creams and sweets. She had with her a list of those girls who had been sent pocket money by their parents. Gezzie and I were never sent a penny by either our mother or our father. So we'd just stand and watch as girl after girl was given sweets or ice cream while we went empty-handed. But there was one young nun, Sister Perpetua, who, when she was in charge of the tray, would let us have some sweets – but only if no one else was looking. That was rare, though.

We slept in enormous dormitories, and it was Sister Perpetua who heard me crying in my bed one night and came over to see what was wrong. I told her I just felt sad. So she went away and returned with a small figurine of the Virgin Mary which she tucked in beside me. 'This'll make you feel better,' she said. 'But I must have it back in the morning.' I went to sleep like a baby, and it's not hard now to see why: I was responding to an almost unknown act of kindness.

The bathing arrangements were beyond belief. Four of us would be made to get into a single large tub together. But we weren't allowed to be naked. First we had to go into a side room where we had to put on little pinafore aprons, tied round our necks and waists and then finished off in a big knot at the back. The idea was that no one else should be able to see our private parts. We were little more than babies, for heaven's sake, but that seemed to count for nothing.

There must have been about a hundred girls at Romsey, with the oldest about eleven. But we weren't treated as children; we were treated as little nuns. And, of course, the sisters didn't give themselves an easy time. We'd hear them crying out in pain as they beat their bare bodies – they called it flagellation – as an act of penance. If an individual nun thought she'd behaved particularly badly or had had impure thoughts, she'd get another of the sisters to beat her to atone for her wickedness. I believed God was benevolent, so why would he allow the nuns to treat the little girls in their care the way we were? If that was something done in the name of religion, I don't want any part of it.

We were woken at 6.30 each morning. As soon as we were dressed, we had to wash round and under our beds. The girl in the first bed had to get a bowl of soapy water and make sure the area round her own bed was clean, then pass it down the line to the next girl. At 7.30 there was half an hour of prayer and then, at last, breakfast. But it was a pretty dismal affair: toast, an apple and a glass of water, never a warm drink. After that, still hungry, we'd go into lessons where the sisters would beat any of us on the slimmest pretext. At one o'clock we were ushered into an enormous hall, like the one in *Oliver!*, and be served plain food: stew or some sort of pie with potatoes, mashed or boiled. But we were never given enough and so we were always hungry. And there was no such thing as fun: for example, we weren't allowed to talk at mealtimes. Why not? The sisters might have taken a vow of silence – but we hadn't.

At 1.30, filing out of the dining hall in a straight line, it was time for another half-hour of praying in the chapel and then back to the classroom. It must feel like that in prison. But the funny thing is that, when I went to the funeral of my husband Pete's mother who'd been a practising Catholic, I knew all the responses, all the hymns. They were so ingrained in me that they rose to the surface all those years later when I needed them.

After more lessons, we broke at 3.50 when we were allowed to play in the fields surrounding the convent – but not before another session of praying. We were outside for an hour and it was wonderful, my favourite time of the day because I felt almost free. There were some swings, although never any toys. In the winter we'd be inside in a huge hall, but there was still a feeling of liberation – or as near as we were ever going to get to it. Evening tea was served around five o'clock after we'd washed our faces and turned down our beds for the night. The meal might be cheese sandwiches and cake, with fruit juice to drink.

Then, whether we were tired or not, we were in bed by seven. The nuns couldn't get rid of us fast enough. Once in bed, we didn't dare make a sound. If any of us did, one of the sisters patrolling the dormitories, twig in hand, would come up to the bed in question and hit us through the blankets. It didn't hurt, but it was intended to be an example to the other little girls. Throughout those miserable days the nuns – apart from Sister Perpetua – showed not one drop of love or tenderness to children who were longing to be in a family environment. It was as if, because the sisters had forsaken everything in their own lives, we shouldn't need anything either.

I'd say to Gezzie, 'We shouldn't be here.' But she was always more accepting than me.

'I know,' she'd reply, 'but we *are* here, aren't we?' Her view was that we just had to get on with it.

Then, for no reason that was ever explained to us, she and I were transferred to the Nazareth House convent in Salisbury, Wiltshire. This was a massive building housing three times as many children, with a brute of a girl called Julia Hyde ruling the roost. Although none of the rest of us was more than eleven or twelve, Julia was sixteen; she'd been there since she was a baby and was the nuns' favourite. But to us she was like a female Flashman, a ruthless bully who took pleasure in hurting and humiliating any children left in her charge. There was a bench in the bathroom where she made us sit and then knocked it over from the back so that we'd all be pitched forwards. Then she'd slap us on our bare bottoms just for the hell of it. The nuns simply turned a blind eye and allowed her to discipline the younger kids as she saw fit.

We only got a change of knickers twice a week. The routine was that a dozen of us at a time would be summoned into the room where all the clothes were laundered. Four nuns would be waiting for us. Then we'd be told to remove our navy blue knickers and turn them inside out, placing the crotch area tightly over one hand. A nun would approach each girl in turn. If any stain whatsoever was detected on the inside of your knickers, you were taken to one side and beaten with one of their twigs across your back or bottom. It was a bewildering, embarrassing and terrifying experience: we couldn't understand why we were being made to feel as though we'd done something wrong. Quite quickly, though, I grew artful. For a couple of days before each inspection I used to stuff wads of toilet paper in the crotch of my knickers in an attempt to absorb any sort of moisture.

What were those nuns up to? Beneath their robes they too were women. What kind of perversion was this? When, many years later, I heard about a group of women of my age suing Nazareth House for the brutal treatment they'd received as children at the hands of those nuns, I could have wept with relief. I hadn't been imagining it all. I wanted to shout from the rooftops to anyone who would listen that those cruel women should never find a place in heaven.

And then one day, without warning, a nun told Gezzie and me to get changed out of our school uniform and into our own clothes. We were taken down to the convent gates, and in walked our mother. I still remember how pretty she looked with her lovely figure and long, slim legs. She didn't mess about, but simply said, 'I'm taking you home.' There were no hugs and kisses – well, not for me, anyway. On the train home, she sat with her arm around Gloria while I pretended to be sleeping on the seat opposite. I was in turmoil, about to swap one hell for another – and, although I was still only six years old, I knew it. It was only later that I found out my mother had won yet another battle with my father. He'd agreed to pay her money for Gezzie, Robert and me – even though Rob wasn't his child – but only on condition that she came and took Gloria and me back to Suffolk Road and paid the rent of not much more than a pound a week. My mother must have been jubilant. It meant that she could live with Mac again, too.

After all that praying on hard wooden benches, I'd developed a painful abscess on my right knee and was limping badly. But, ignoring my plight, my mother went out as soon as we got back home. Grandma Mary was there, however, and she knew something was wrong with me. When I showed her my knee she put a warm bread poultice on it which drew out the poison and relieved the pain. It left a big scar, visible to this day and a constant reminder of those wretched months in the care of those appalling women.

5

Mind Games

My mother would get up in the morning at any time between eight and eleven, depending on her mood and how much drink she'd had the night before. It was up to Gloria and me to get ourselves up, washed, dressed and off to school with a bowl of cereal or a piece of toast and Marmite inside us. As often as not, Gloria would walk to school with me. But after we finished in the afternoon I usually walked home alone.

I wore a white cotton shirt under a sleeveless navy gymslip with big pleats in the skirt, back and front. As soon as I got indoors I'd take it off, hold down the pleats with big, loose tacking stitches, iron it and hang it over my chair in the bedroom. I was so tiny, I could hardly reach the ironing board. The following morning, I'd remove each tacking stitch and the pleats would be lying flat. I wanted to look smart.

My mother took me to school only once

throughout my entire education: on my first day, aged five, when I started in the infants. Every step I took up Suffolk Road was torture. I've never liked unknown places, then or now. And I hated the idea of going to this new place called school; unfortunately, my instinct proved accurate. There was nothing particularly wrong with the school; it's just that I felt like a fish out of water. I also instinctively knew that I wouldn't make friends because I didn't know how. Life at home was so dreadful that I'd never learnt the art of socialising. To this day, I'll always find an excuse not to walk into a room full of strangers if I'm on my own. It's not helped by the fact that my eyesight is poor, which makes it difficult to see the faces in front of me. As a child at school I couldn't see the blackboard properly. Gloria had been born with a very severe squint in one eye which had been corrected by an operation. But if my mother noticed the squint in *my* eye she certainly never did anything about it – I was never taken for an eye test.

Years later, when I was nineteen and living in Liverpool, I got a job working on an assembly line at the Meccano factory. I kept missing the drill that was meant to cut a hole in the wheel of a toy car coming down the conveyor belt, and repeatedly cut myself instead. Eventually, the supervisor sent me to the nurse who bandaged my bloody fingers and then gave me an eye test. It turned out that I was virtually blind in my right eye and short-sighted in my left. I was then given two days' paid leave to sort myself out and go for a proper eye test with a trained optician, who gave me a prescription for glasses. Meccano paid for them in the first instance and docked my wages at source until they were repaid. When I returned to the factory, I was moved to a job in the packing department. Little wonder I hadn't been able to see the blackboard at school!

The Truant Inspector was a frequent visitor at our house to ask my mother why her daughters weren't attending school on a regular basis. And she'd lie and say, 'Well, I don't know because I send them off each morning.' I don't know whether he believed her, but most people did. She would have made a very good actress. Not that it always did the trick. When the authorities started asking awkward questions, my mother did what she always did: she went on the attack. For her, it was the best line of defence. She'd be up at the school loudly demanding to see the head, Miss Bonnie, who looked a bit like the Queen Mother, portly and rather pretty. Gloria was a constant problem at school, falling out with both teachers and pupils, and then she'd be called in to see the head for a ticking-off. Our mother wasn't having any of that. She'd stride up

Suffolk Road swinging her arms all hoity-toity, march into Milton Road School and go straight into Miss Bonnie's office.

'How dare you speak to my daughter like that!' she'd shout. 'Why should she come to your school if that's how you treat her?'

Eventually it got to the point where Miss Bonnie and Gloria's teachers couldn't stand it a moment longer. Miss Bonnie simply couldn't reason with my mother, so inspectors would call at the house. And, in the end, my mother always won. They just couldn't take the insults and, rather than provoke another tirade for some perfectly justified complaint about Gloria's behaviour or our absences, they decided that saying nothing was preferable. My mother was trouble and they didn't want any of it. Better to admit defeat and move on.

Those were different times. People claim these days that the authorities intervene too much, that we're living in a nanny state, and I understand that feeling. But as I look back now, I do wonder that no teacher spotted a child crying out for help and love and some sort of support. No teacher ever took me to one side and said, 'What's up?' Yes, I was well-behaved and quiet, but surely I must have struck someone as a strange, troubled child? But then again, the war wasn't long over and many people had enough trouble just getting from one day to the next. They'd lost loved ones, their homes had been bombed and many things were still rationed. I suppose people had too many difficulties of their own to have time for mine. I wouldn't have been able to express it like this back then, but just remained isolated in my own unhappy little bubble. Emotionally, I was threadbare. I never mixed with the other kids. I'd stand and drink my free milk at playtime on my own. I had a terrible attendance record. I'd given up on life – and I was still only at junior school.

I was, therefore, on my own, responsible for myself. I quickly came to realise that you couldn't expect people to help you – you had to help yourself. Yet I was young and powerless. I had no independence, no money. I had to rely on my mother for everything. And that included love – of which I received none. Abuse and neglect are a terrible combination.

Like everything else in my miserable life, it was all down to my mother. Her reputation had spread across the city. No one wanted to tackle her: she was big trouble. If helping me meant locking horns with her, who in their right mind would? I think most people who might have been aware – the teachers, the newspaper delivery boy, the milkman – took the line of least resistance and convinced themselves it wasn't their problem. After all, even Miss Bonnie had given up on her – and she was a pillar of the community. My mother could be very disruptive as she ranted and raved at Miss Bonnie; everyone could hear her. Why would anyone else want to get involved? And why would anyone else start fighting my corner? No one wanted to cross swords with my mother; and that included my father – unless, of course, he could get one over on her.

Social Services, as we now know the concept, didn't exist then. And even today, in the age of the social worker, you read horror stories of children who've somehow dropped through the gaps in the system. After the war there wasn't even a system. And my mother was no fool. Even when drunk she'd belt me on my elbows, on my back and across the backs of my legs – all places that were covered by clothes, so no one was ever going to see any bruises there. She'd slap me round the face, but the bright pink marks would fade after about an hour. I would never have told a teacher about my rotten home life, either – I wouldn't have dared. I developed a sixth sense: things were bad enough without inviting more trouble. It's why at an early age I gave up on living and just concentrated on one thing: surviving.

My mother may have been reckless with whatever money she could lay her hands on, cigarettes and drink topping her list of priorities. But she was nobody's fool when it came to getting as much as she could out of anyone who came her way, my father being the main contributor. Every so often she'd decide she wanted him to give her more money, and that's when the trouble would start all over again.

When I was seven, and living again in Suffolk Road, she put renewed pressure on him. At first he refused, so she employed her old trick of using Gezzie and me to embarrass him. He was stationed at Eastney Barracks at the time, and we were sent up there to ask the guard on the gate if we could see him. When my father eventually appeared, looking shiny as a new pin in his smart uniform, he was bright red with embarrassment. He was a proud man and a private one, too. My mother had won because she'd made him look foolish. He wasn't going through this little charade again, so he gave Gezzie and me some money on the spot to get her, and us, off his back. My unspoken dream of somehow getting away from Suffolk Road – don't ask me how I thought I'd manage it – had suffered one more blow.

My parents must have divorced not long after this, but even that turned into a sort of vicious game. I can still remember my mother's fury. 'That fucking bastard,' she exclaimed one day. 'He's applied for custody of you two girls and Rob, and he's only fucking got it!' My father was divorcing her on the grounds of her adultery with Mac, and in those days an adulterous woman was considered very sinful. Dad was still back and forth, fighting in Malaya, so it wasn't as though he could look after us kids – he just wanted to spite my mother.

The judge declared her to be a fallen woman, and my father revelled in her public humiliation. He knew she'd have to continue looking after us – she wanted to keep the house, and she needed his Admiralty allowance to help pay the rent. But that was no reason, from his point of view, not to make a little mischief along the way. And so it went on: each of them playing games and scoring points off each other, with Gezzie, Rob and me stuck in the middle. My mother would usually send me to the post office to collect the Admiralty allowance and as often as not, as I set off up the road, she'd tell me, 'I don't want you but the money comes in handy.' It was one of her favourite sayings.

I was always a very feminine little girl, interested in my mother's cosmetics and perfumes. She was fond of something called Evening in Paris which came in a mauve bottle. It was cheap, but I thought it smelt lovely. She kept it in the living room. One day, I decided to open the bottle and dab some of the scent behind my ears. Then I panicked, because I was sure she'd notice that the level had gone down. So I thought I'd top it up with water.

The liquid immediately turned white and cloudy. I went frantic – she'd notice that immediately. I got a chair, climbed on to it and threw the bottle to the very back of a high, window ledge. Then I scrubbed and scrubbed behind my ears with toilet paper soaked in water. I was sure she'd smell the perfume on me if I got too close. Of course, in time she noticed the bottle was missing – but for some reason she didn't accuse me. For days I was terrified that she'd find the bottle, but on this occasion I was lucky.

I wasn't usually so fortunate. Sometimes, past caring, I'd answer her back and then I knew I'd get a lashing. One day she gave me a ten shilling note to go to the corner shop. 'Get me ten Woodbines,' she said. 'No, make it twenty plus a quarter of spam cut thin and a loaf.'

I don't know why I was so daft, but I turned and said, 'Why are you buying cigarettes? With that money we could have beans and potatoes to go with the spam, and maybe a cake.'

I thought she'd explode. She drew back her hand and slapped me as hard as she could across the face. 'Get to the fucking shops!' she screamed.

A good day was a day when she didn't hit me. But since I never knew when that was going to be I could never relax, never just do the things children like to do, because I was always in fear of sudden flare-ups. And as there was no one I could confide in, there was never a time when I didn't feel lonely or anxious. If you're born into a house without love, it takes you years to realise what you haven't got.

I'd arrive back from school on days when I'd been fit enough to attend and come into the house as quietly as possible. I needed to gauge the mood before I changed out of my school clothes and got on with the chores my mother needed doing. Throughout my childhood I wore the same kind of things every day: a blouse, a sweater, a skirt – girls never wore trousers in those days – socks and shoes. But the tradition was that all the kids in the street would get dressed up for Sunday, and Gezzie and I would wear gingham dresses with puffed sleeves and patent shoes.

Sunday was also the day when every family would have a roast meal, usually chicken in our house. For the rest of the week there'd be tea at about 4.30, with everyone, including my mother, sitting at the kitchen table. It was never anything fancy: spam or corned beef sandwiches, digestive biscuits and a mug of tea or a glass of lemonade. If money was tight – usually on Wednesdays, because Thursday was pay day – it would be jam sandwiches.

There wasn't homework back then, so after tea,

if the weather was fine, I'd go into the street with my skipping rope or play with marbles in the gutter. Sometimes I'd go to Bransbury Park; in the winter. I'd just stay in the bedroom Gloria and I shared. Every so often Uncle Gordon – my mother's younger brother – would be on leave from the Merchant Navy. He'd come round to our house, and Gezzie and I would always do the same thing for him: we'd clean out a jam jar and then go looking for discarded cigarette butts in the street. Everyone smoked, it seemed, in those days, and there were no filter cigarettes then. When the jam jar was full to the brim with dog-ends, we'd put the lid on and take it back to Uncle Gordon. He'd empty the ends on to a newspaper, remove the bits of cigarette paper, mash all the loose tobacco together and then roll himself as many cigarettes as he could. Gezzie and I would be given a few pennies for our troubles. I'd trot up the road to Gilbert's shop and buy two ounces of Knobbly Nuts for threepence. They were like pink popcorn and very light, so two ounces filled a large bag.

As I got older – ten or eleven – Gloria and I would have to get the younger children to bed. My mother never bothered, and anyway she'd be too drunk by then. There was also all their ironing to be done. Having washed myself as best I could at the kitchen sink I wouldn't get into my own bed until about nine – much too late for a child my age. I'd always send up a silent prayer that I'd be able to sleep through the night without my mother and Mac having a screaming row and Gezzie and me being ordered downstairs so we could witness her humiliating him.

My lack of friends wasn't just down to my inability to make relationships; it was also partly deliberate, because I knew I could never bring anyone home. There'd be no telling how my mother would behave, and in any case other children's parents wouldn't have allowed them to come to such a bad house. Very occasionally, though, I'd be invited to other houses, and that's when I realised what I was missing. Daphne and Delphine Scott were non-identical twins in my class. Daphne was chubby; Delphine was thin. They lived opposite my junior school, and sometimes I'd go to their house for an ice cream after school. The girls were their mother's pride and joy, her only children, and she doted on them. The home was warm and loving. As soon as we got indoors, the twins' mother would kiss them and then tell them to go and change out of their school clothes. After a happy and relaxed tea, their dad would come back from work and they'd run to him and hug each other. At such moments I felt especially sad and lonely: this was everything I longed for.

Every so often I also went to play with a girl called Joan Richards, who lived seven doors up on the other side of Suffolk Road. Her father was American, and he only came home occasionally. I sensed a sadness in the mother. I don't think things were right between Joan's mum and dad. But I felt more comfortable in that environment than in Daphne and Delphine's because it wasn't totally happy. It meant that Joan and I had something in common.

Apart from the infants, all my schools were single-sex. I barely knew any boys of my own age, and for some reason I was frightened of them. At one stage I developed a bit of a crush on a boy called Robin Fell who lived locally, just opposite the hospital. He was a very good-looking boy and slowly we started talking to each other. I'd go round to his house and sit on his front wall, chatting to him. The other girls used to tease me. They'd chant:

> Robin Fell, where did he fall?
> Right over Pat McKenzie's wall!

It probably lasted no more than a few weeks, but I liked being with such a handsome boy. It made me feel less rejected.

When I was eight, my mother was pregnant with Mac's third child, Neil. Just as she was about to give birth Mac became ill, bent almost double with pain. But no one knew why. Finally he collapsed, and Dr Powell diagnosed a duodenal ulcer. Mac was rushed into hospital. When he came home, he had to lie on his front for weeks and could only eat boiled food. Mother had given birth in the meantime, but Mac couldn't really help her – and in those days women stayed in bed for up to two weeks after they'd had a baby.

As a result of all this there was no one to look after Gezzie, Robert and me, so for three or four weeks we were placed in somewhere called the Cottage Homes in the grounds of a large estate in Cosham, not far from where we lived. But for all that it was a break from our troubled home, from the screaming and the beatings, I felt adrift and unhappy. From this distance, I can see that being in Suffolk Road was, as I'd felt in the earlier foster homes and children's homes, the lesser of two evils. Going to the Cottage Homes was yet another major upheaval, which wasn't properly explained to me. Having said that, I do remember that everyone was very kind and I did enjoy the peace. Not that it was to last for long.

Only a matter of weeks later, my father made one of his rare appearances. He was very tanned from being in Malaya, but that's not why I remember this particular visit. For the first and last time, he'd brought presents for us all. And not just any old present – he gave each of us girls a brand-new bicycle and Rob a green wooden crocodile. He must have bought the bikes from the shop at the top of the road and then wheeled them down Suffolk Road to our front door. I couldn't believe that this was happening to me. Gloria's bike was black, mine a beautiful pale green, with a silver bell and a basket at the front. I was thrilled. I'd never owned anything so valuable in my entire life.

I didn't even know how to ride a bike! But my father taught me in the street that very day. I was so excited I thought I was going to faint. I washed and polished my bike every day till it was gleaming, and then I'd ride round the local streets in every spare minute I had. For a solitary child like me, a bike was ideal. It gave me something to do that I loved and didn't involve other children.

About six months later, when I arrived home from school one day, my mother was waiting for me. 'I'm going to get you and Gloria new bikes,' she said. I didn't know what she was talking about. I didn't need a new bike; I already had a perfectly good one. 'Never mind that,' she said. 'I want you and Gloria to bring your bikes with me to the Eastney cycle shop now.' I must have looked confused. 'Just do as you're told!' she shouted.

I couldn't argue, but I knew something bad was going to happen. Gloria was walking beside her, wheeling her bike and not batting an eyelid. I was trailing behind, my heart hammering in my chest. When we got to the bike shop my mother went inside with Gloria and started talking to the man behind the counter. I hung back in the doorway with my bike which meant I couldn't quite make out what they were saying, but I kept hearing her say something like, 'No, I can't do that. No, I couldn't manage that.' Then she called over to me to bring my bike in and leave it next to the counter.

Eventually she and Gloria came out of the shop, but empty-handed. I was beginning to panic now.

'Where's my bike?' I asked.

My mother looked at me. 'I've sold it,' she replied, 'and Gloria's, too.'

I couldn't believe what I was hearing.

'But I didn't need a new one,' I said, aghast.

She just ignored that as she and Gloria crossed the road and started walking home. I trailed behind, totally broken-hearted.

Sitting on the wall outside our house, not knowing what to do with myself, I couldn't understand the cruelty. I'd have begged and cried if I'd thought my mother would listen. But I knew she wouldn't – she couldn't have cared less about my feelings. And, of course, she never did get round to replacing my pride and joy. It was only many years later, as a grown woman, that I reminded Gloria of that incident. Apparently, our mother was in arrears with the rent as usual, and needed some money fast. Then she'd hit on the idea of selling our bikes. But she hadn't been able to afford to leave a deposit on two new ones – especially as Gloria's was by then getting a bit battered – so she'd just taken all the money for herself.

And yet, despite everything she'd done to me, I never stopped trying to win my mother's love. As a child, I could see that she was cold and vicious – but I was confused. I still couldn't work out what I'd done to be treated like this. I thought it must somehow be my fault. Perhaps if I did more things for her, she'd grow fond of me. Or that's how I reasoned it in my head.

When she was twenty-nine – so I must have been almost ten – I saved up to buy her a birthday present. An old lady who lived at the top of Suffolk Road had called out to me one day when I was walking home from school. Would I mind going to the Jug and Bottle to fill up her soda siphon? She said she'd give me a few pennies for my trouble. The trip to the off-licence became a regular errand, and it meant I built up a tiny nest egg. It's how I saved up enough money to be able to buy my mother a present.

I had found a brooch I liked in a local shop. It was imitation gold, shaped like a bow of ribbon with a small hook from which hung a little book. If you unhooked the book, it unravelled to reveal a series of views of Britain's favourite beauty spots. I thought it was the prettiest thing I'd ever seen. It probably cost no more than two shillings, but that was all the money I had. I'd gone without my sweets for weeks until I could afford it, and I was thrilled. I remember running home to give it to my mother.

I can see her now. It was 23 February 1952, and she was standing in the living room in a Norman Hartnell dress. He was the designer who dressed the Queen and the Queen Mother, but ordinary members of the public could buy cheap copies from catalogues. This particular dress was brown with three-quarter-length sleeves, a fitted waist with a belt and a flared skirt. There was a frilly white bib at the front which was detachable to make it easier for washing. My mother had put on a bit of weight in her twenties but she still looked good, her hair worn long and glossy, her nails immaculate and painted her favourite shade of red. Proudly, I handed her the brooch.

'Oh, thank you,' she said, and pinned it on. Then she started talking to Gloria.

From that day, I never saw it again. I didn't ask her where it was: I didn't want to hear the answer. She never referred to it again, and I was simply too hurt to say anything.

I was never a naughty child – I was clean and tidy and well-behaved. I may have been shown only cruelty by my mother, but that never encouraged me to be cruel myself. On the contrary, I've always considered myself to be a kind person; I truly believe that's how I came into this world and that's how I will go out of it. But the way I was mistreated by her did gradually begin to affect how I behaved towards her. The first stirrings of rebellion started to rise up in me.

I'd been beaten and neglected, starved of love and affection, more or less from the day I was born. But some incidents cut deeper than others, and they didn't necessarily involve physical abuse. I was a member of the local Brownies, who met in a hut in Eastney and put on a nativity play at Christmas to which the children's families were invited. One year – it must have been at the beginning of the 1950s – I was cast as the Angel Gabriel. I'd had to miss a couple of rehearsals after bad beatings from my mother, and sometimes she'd tell me I couldn't go just for the hell of it. 'You're not going if I say you're not,' she'd shout. It was a form of mental torture every bit as painful as being physically abused by her. But I was determined not to miss the actual performance, at which the Lady Mayoress of Portsmouth was to be guest of honour. My mother had always gone to see Gloria in any production put on by her school or the Brownies, and so I assumed she'd come to mine. Someone had made me a white smock and a pair of wings. I'd learned my lines and I knew I was word perfect. I'd also been to enough rehearsals to know where to stand and when to move.

On the day of the performance I was so excited when I woke up. I couldn't wait to get out of school and into my costume. I loved the idea of escaping, however briefly, into someone else's identity, and I don't mind admitting that the thought of performing in front of a real-life audience was a huge thrill. I wasn't nervous at all, although it did feel like being in a dream. I was just walking on stage when Brown Owl suddenly hissed, 'Take your socks off!' I'd forgotten to remove my grey woollen socks which had holes in the heels – we called them spuds – when I put on my costume. As a little girl, I could just about remember my mother being a dab hand at darning. But, like so much else, that had gone by the board years ago. I quickly removed my socks and threw them out of sight.

Taking up my position, I remember peering into the audience to see if I could spot my mother anywhere. No sign of her. I couldn't understand it. She'd said she'd be there. But the performance was about to begin, and very soon it was my turn to speak. 'Hail Mary!' I declaimed. 'Peace be unto thee. I am the Angel of the Lord to whom all things art known. Thou art favoured among women, Mary, and the blessing of the Lord is upon thee.' I felt so proud – next stop Hollywood, surely!

Now I had a chance to scan the audience again. But, hard as I looked, I still couldn't see my mother. It had been a wonderful moment and I wanted her to have seen it. The Lady Mayoress had obviously noticed me, though. She approached me afterwards, a tall woman with wavy grey hair and wearing a tweed pencil skirt with matching jacket, a beautiful rope of pearls and pointy-toed shoes. She also had on her chain of office. 'That was wonderful, child,' she said in ringing tones. 'We heard every word.' Years later I realised she sounded just like Dame Edith Evans as Lady Bracknell in *The Importance of Being Earnest*. At the time I just felt like the bees' knees.

And *still* my mother was nowhere to be seen. All the other parents were congratulating their daughters but I just stood there, the only child on her own. I remember feeling overwhelmed with sadness. Why wouldn't my own mother want to see me? Why wouldn't she be proud like the other mothers and fathers? I watched the other kids being hugged and just thought, *I have to escape from this*. And yet I had nowhere to go. I knew I had to stay with her for several more years – I was still only ten – but I hated my mother at that moment in a way a child should never hate its parent.

It was a turning point. As I walked back down the road to our house, I tried hard not to cry. I knew I'd been good. I'd remembered my lines and spoken them well. And she couldn't even be bothered to be there for my moment of triumph. I walked through the front door and there she was in the kitchen, drinking. She looked at me as I came in.

'Why didn't you come?' I asked.

'I did,' she told me. 'I was there but I left early.'

'No, you didn't,' I remonstrated.

She took a puff of her cigarette. 'Oh, you can think what you fucking well like,' she said dismissively.

I just couldn't believe it. I walked out of the room, ran up to my bedroom and lay curled up on my bed, and oh, did I sob. Any feelings I might still have had for her were gone forever. At that moment I knew that she was a truly rotten mother. At that moment I grew up.

In some ways, my mother's emotional abuse was actually worse than when she hit me physically. Bruises heal. Mental scars never fade. She didn't care what pain she inflicted on my body, and the same was true of my mind. Today, I can't remember most of the beatings I suffered as a child; most of them just blend into one. But I can't forget the other ways in which she hurt me.

Just before we left Suffolk Road – so I wasn't yet quite eleven – Grandma Mary gave Gezzie and me each a glass container in the shape of a bunch of grapes, filled with green toilet water. They were Christmas presents which she could barely afford. I thought mine was the most gorgeous thing I'd ever seen in my life. When her bottle was empty, Gloria threw it away. But I kept mine as a prized possession. Once I'd used all the toilet water, I washed out the bottle and put it on a doily on the dressing-table in our bedroom. The light would shine through the window on to it and it looked beautiful.

One day I came home from school, went straight upstairs and took the bottle off the dressing-table. It fascinated me, but then I loved anything feminine. Just as I was putting it back, my mother came up the stairs and walked into the room. I could tell she'd been drinking.

'Why didn't you come and say hello when you got back from school?' she demanded.

I told her that I'd just wanted to play with the bottle Grandma had given me for Christmas. But I could tell there was going to be trouble – I'd developed a sixth sense for it.

'What fucking bottle?' she said, looking round the room.

I tried saying that I'd been just about to come down to see her, but it was too late – she'd spotted my treasure. She moved over to the dressing-table, picked up the bottle and hurled it as hard as she could at the iron fireplace. It smashed into a thousand pieces. Then she turned to me. 'Well, you won't be able to play with your bottle again, will you, you little cow?'

I looked at her, my mouth hanging open, tears welling in my eyes.

'Oh, and another thing,' she added, 'make sure you fucking clear up all this mess.' Then she walked out of the room.

I fell on to the bed and cried so hard that I made my eyes sore. But what could I do? I had to walk down to the kitchen, get a pan and brush and sweep up all the fragments from my precious bottle. If not, there'd be more trouble from my mother. As I returned with the pan of broken glass to empty it into the bin, I could feel her watching me. 'That'll fucking teach you to ignore me when you get home,' she snarled. At that moment, I loathed that woman with all of my heart.

6

Moving On

The only subject I was good at was English, but it wasn't enough to get me into grammar school. I sat my 11+ but I didn't stand a chance. I remember coming home the day I'd been told I hadn't passed. My mother was sitting there with Gloria, smoking. 'Well,' she said, 'how did you go on?' She knew the results had been due that day. I told her I'd failed. She looked straight at me and said, 'I thought you'd have passed. You're bright.' How I kept quiet, I don't know. I wanted to say, 'How did you expect me to pass? I hardly ever go to school because you ill-treat me. I'm desperately unhappy. How could I have passed?' But I knew to keep my thoughts to myself.

As a general rule, my mother never asked me how my day had been at school, never showed any interest whatsoever in my lessons or how I was getting on. I'd walk through the door and she'd say, 'Don't bother taking your coat off.' She always needed something from the shops, so off I'd go and do as I was told. If I hadn't, I'd have got a hiding. Pity she didn't take as much interest in my schooling as she did in getting another packet of cigarettes or bottle of VP port wine. She didn't come to a single parents' evening throughout my entire education.

Gloria didn't go to school much, either, although for rather different reasons. She would offer to stay off school to clean the house and help look after baby Robert. Mother loved that. She liked Gezzie's company and she liked the house looking nice. And Gloria didn't care whether she went to school or not. I'd have loved to have had a proper education but there wasn't a week throughout my childhood when I ever went to school on five consecutive days. I was too often either nursing my bruises or sleeping off the effects of another night of fights and dramas.

By now, I was becoming mature enough to make comparisons with other girls. And it was increasingly obvious to me that my mother had turned her children into social outcasts. No one wanted anything to do with the McKenzie or McGinley kids. On top of that, she despised me. I had gradually come to the realisation that this wasn't just my mind working overtime. This was the reality and something she reminded me of on an almost daily basis. But that didn't mean it wasn't hard to take.

Grandma Mary was kind to me when she could be, but she had troubles enough with raising my Uncle Neville single-handed, and anyway there were long periods when my mother wouldn't allow her in the house after yet another screaming match. All the time I was being ill-treated by my mother, Gloria would look the other way or tell me to stop crying all the time. Uncle Neville was still just a lad when I was growing up, preoccupied with football and girls. Anyway, I'm pretty certain he wouldn't have been aware of what was going on at Suffolk Road. And he couldn't have stood up to my mother, even if it had occurred to him to do so.

The situation was hopeless, and I had no choice but to face it on my own. So I lived in a fantasy world to block out the reality. I spent as much time as possible in my room reading the *Girl's Crystal* magazine and something called the *Hollywood Album*, all about American film stars. I knew it made sense to keep my head down, because one day I'd be free. But it was a long time to wait until I was sixteen, the earliest age at which young people could leave home. I was ill-educated – hardly surprising since I'd missed so much schooling – so I didn't even have the prospect of getting a decent job when I left school at fifteen. If I could have done, I'd have been able to save some money and then maybe I could have broken free.

As I was rising eleven, although I didn't know it my time in Suffolk Road was about to come to an end for ever. It was a private house with a rent of one pound ten shillings a week, cheap even by 1950s' standards. It was certainly an amount my mother could easily afford. She was receiving eight shillings a week family allowance for me, Robert, Neil and baby Penny who'd been born the previous year (although nothing for Gloria, because the state didn't pay out for the first child). She was also getting the money Mac paid her each week from his job painting the liners in Southampton Docks. On Thursdays he'd hand over his brown pay packet unopened – that was the tradition in those days – and then she'd hand him back enough money for his beer and bits and pieces. (Once a week, on his way home, he'd call in at Gilbert's, the sweet shop that's still there at the top of the road, and buy something for Gloria, me, Rob and Neil.) On top of that, my mother got a generous weekly allowance from the Admiralty for Gloria, me and Rob. Compared with some people in the road we must have been quite well off.

My mother, then, could well have afforded to pay the rent on the house, and yet she fell further and further behind. Her own needs always came first. The money went on cigarettes, booze at home and in the pubs around Portsmouth, make-up, perfume, nail varnish – you name it. And although she didn't have lots of clothes she always made sure she had a nice coat to go out in, and you'd never see her in a pair of old shoes. It was different for us kids. The shoes I had to wear to school were so worn down that I was embarrassed. The backs were splayed out so that from behind they looked like mules, and I always imagined the other kids were laughing at me as I walked past. That's why, to this day, if there's even a scratch on one of my shoes I'll throw them out.

I never saw my mother pay the rent, so perhaps she used to hand the money in at an office somewhere. But I do remember the letters that used to come through the door telling her she was in arrears. I was getting old enough to understand what that meant – if she got too far behind, we'd be thrown out of the house. And that scared me. Where would we go? I was miserable in Suffolk Road but at least I had the security of a roof over my head with my own bed and my few possessions around me. Was all that about to change?

Then another thought crossed my mind. There was a girl in the same class as me at Milton School who'd been fostered and who lived in Bransbury Road. Sometimes, on the way back from school, I'd pop into her house and I could see for myself that this was a nice family. I knew the authorities wouldn't allow children to be left homeless, I'd be put with a foster family too. I hadn't much liked the various homes I'd been farmed out to when I was younger, true, but if I had the good luck to be placed with the kind of family I had seen in Bransbury Road that *had* to be better than staying with my mother.

At all events, my instinct that we were about to move on was correct. When she first got behind with the rent, my mother would pay part of what she owed. But then she'd let it slide again until it got really bad. And so the pattern would be repeated. But by Christmas 1952, three months before my eleventh birthday, the situation had become serious. I know because I saw the letter saying she was now months and months in arrears. But being in debt didn't seem to bother her. And Mac never said anything – not in my hearing, anyway. He could have taken money from his own wage packet and started to pay the back rent. But that would have started another row and all he wanted, what we all wanted, was a quiet life. I remember Mac sitting down on the sofa on one occasion after yet another fight between him and my mother. 'Pat,' he said to her, 'why can't we just have peace?' It didn't seem too much to ask.

In January 1953 – I remember because it was freezing cold – my mother saw an advert in the local paper for caravans to rent. They were at a site on the other side of Bransbury Park, near Southsea Beach and about a mile from where we lived. She went up there and rented two of them, one large, one small. Under more and more pressure from the landlord of Suffolk Road to make a dent in her debt, she'd promised him faithfully that she'd pay everything she owed by the end of January – but in fact she hadn't any intention of doing so. That evening I overheard her saying to Mac, 'I'm not paying that man any fucking money. We're doing a moonlight flit tomorrow first thing.'

Despite my anxiety about what would happen if we had to leave Suffolk Road, when I heard we were moving to a caravan I wasn't upset but excited. Caravans were to do with holidays, weren't they? This was a distraction from my miserable little life, something a bit different. Maybe things were going to get better after all.

My mother was crafty – I'll give her that. Next, she borrowed the local rag and bone man's hand-cart to transport our bits and pieces to the caravan site. The next morning she got Gezzie and me out of our beds at five o'clock and made us help her load up this cart with pots and pans, the ironing board, bedding, all sorts. Then she told us to wheel it to the site. It was heavy work and we had to take care the cart didn't tip over and spill everything on to the street. But we made it there safely, amid fits of hysterical giggles, and then went all the way back to Suffolk Road to get the next load.

The caravans were fully furnished so we didn't need all our old furniture, which my mother sold to a second-hand shop. That gave her a nice little sum to pay the rent on the caravans. And, as she must have guessed, the landlord of Suffolk Road never came after her for the arrears of rent. I should think he was glad to see the back of her, just like the neighbours.

Furnished they may have been, but even so our two new homes were pretty basic. Certainly, there were no fancy fixtures and fittings. The larger one was for my mother, Mac, Rob, Neil and baby Penny. Gloria and I got the smaller caravan. We could have stayed put indefinitely, but my mother had her eye on something better. Some of the caravans were summer rentals only and rather luxurious. Living about a hundred yards from us was a lady called Morag McCrea who owned seven of these smarter caravans, and my mother – using all her guile and cunning – made it her business to become friendly with her. Mrs McCrea knew none of the history of Suffolk Road and, anyway my mother could charm the birds out of the trees if she wanted something badly enough. The role she chose for herself on this occasion was that of a posh woman who'd fallen on hard times, and Mrs McCrea fell for it. Her seven caravans were booked up for summer lets from the end of May, but it was still only the end of February and I think she was pleased to get a bit of extra money from allowing our family to live in one of them. 'Anyway,' she said, 'I don't like to see you and your four children and that poor little baby living in such scruffy conditions.' So she let us have one of her beautiful caravans. It had chintz curtains, proper carpeting – everything you could want. But she made my mother promise to move out by the end of May.

Our new home had enough room to sleep all of us. My mother and Mac had a single bed each and then there was a double bed; Gezzie and I slept at one end, Rob and Neil at the other. Little Penny slept in a separate crib. There was a built-in kitchen with a pull-out table and little benches. Unlike the first two caravans this one was lovely and warm, with its own Calor gas stove. The roof stood on a sort of raised section about ten inches above the four walls. The whole arrangement seemed like the height of luxury to me.

During the day I'd go to school, but the end of my education, if you can call it that, was in sight. Gloria and I were both sent to a secondary modern a short walk away. The only memory I have of that school is that in the brief time I was there I got a crush on Barbara Rush, the head girl. Lovely to look at, with dark, glossy hair and tanned skin, she was clever and very good at sport too. She had it all, and everybody loved her. I so wanted to be Barbara Rush. I'd hang around outside the school gates until she came out, but I didn't dare go near her or talk to her. As she walked off, however, I'd shout out her name and then run away. She was everything I wasn't.

Although my mother carried on drinking, she never once hit me while we lived on that caravan site. She'd row with Mac, of course – that was never going to change; but she never took it out on me. She knew we were surrounded by other caravans with thin walls like our own, so she couldn't get away with knocking a child about because everyone would be able to hear. Grandma Mary had said my mother wasn't mad but evil. And maybe she was right. If she wanted to control herself, she could.

Even so, the adventure of living in a caravan soon wore off. We were like rats in a cage and it all became too much. My mother was at Mac the whole time, and then he'd go storming off and she'd hit the bottle even harder. And she always had some scam or other up her sleeve. She noticed that some people had milk delivered to their caravans each morning, and she reckoned she could save a bit of money there. Gezzie and I were ordered to go and steal bottles of milk from them. She'd send us out early, before we went to school, and I always tried to get out of it because it made me feel really uncomfortable. I knew we were doing wrong and I pleaded with her not to make us do it – I hated the idea of stealing. But she wouldn't listen. 'Get out there,' she insisted, 'and get me some fucking milk.' Most parents, I came to realise as I grew up, teach their children the difference between right and wrong. Not my mother. Her attitude was that everybody owed her.

This went on for about two weeks. I was certain we'd be caught in the end – and, sure enough, we were. We used to steal the milk from outside the caravan of one of our neighbours, although not one that was too close. Being kids, we didn't have the sense to steal from a variety of caravans. After he kept missing his milk the man who lived there set a trap for us and then called the police. When the bobby turned up our mother pretended she had no idea what we'd been up to. 'I don't know what my daughters were thinking,' she said. The policeman asked her, in that case, where she had thought all the milk was coming from. 'Oh, I don't know,' she replied, and you could see him thinking it just wasn't worth doing battle with this woman.

We weren't prosecuted, though, but just taken

down to the police station and told that if we ever did this again we'd be in trouble. I was shocked and deeply upset, on edge the whole time. Each morning I'd wake up fearing what this new day would bring. There just didn't seem to be any way my life was going to get better. One day, I turned to Gloria. 'This is horrible,' I said. 'I can't stand it any longer. I'm leaving.' She asked me where I was going. I told her I didn't know and I didn't care. 'Anywhere away from here.' To my surprise she said she'd come with me – the only time I can remember Gezzie ganging up with me against our mother.

I had a little money put by from babysitting for a pretty woman called Pauline, with two children and no husband, who lived in the caravan a few doors down from ours. She liked to go out a couple of nights a week with her boyfriend, and had asked me to keep an eye on her kids. My mother had said I could as long as I gave her some of the money. So, with the help of my little nest egg, Gloria and I hatched a plan. Instead of going to school one morning, we caught a bus to the local station and hopped on the first train that came in. It turned out to be going to London. Heaven knows what we thought we were going to do when we got there, but we felt full of excitement and trepidation.

After about an hour, though, the train pulled

into a station and a policeman got on board. Gezzie and I sank lower and lower into our seats as he got nearer and nearer. We weren't in school uniform – you didn't wear one at our secondary school – so we didn't think he'd notice us particularly. But when he reached us, he stopped. In a kind voice, he said, 'Are you Gloria and Pat McKenzie?'

In unison we squeaked, 'No!'

He winked at us. 'Come on, girls,' he said. 'We're getting off.'

To this day I don't know how the police were on to us so quickly. Maybe the school told them we were missing. What I do know is that we were up to our eyeballs in trouble. During the journey on the way back to the caravan site in a police car I was absolutely terrified. My mother was going to give me the hidng of my life and I couldn't escape it. I didn't have enough money to run away for good, and I didn't know anyone else well enough to go and stay in their house. I'd have given anything in the whole wide world not to have to walk back into that caravan. But I had no choice.

When we arrived we just waited for the balloon to go up. But the bobby was with us and so, quick as a flash, our mother swung into a convincing pretence of being all concerned and worried and relieved that her little girls had been found safe and sound. When he'd gone I prepared myself for the worst, but amazingly she just gave us sandwiches which we ate in silence and then we were sent to bed. Nor did she lash out later on. What we'd done was never mentioned. I suppose she still felt inhibited by the closeness of the other caravans and their listening occupants. If she could have got away with it I'd have been well and truly beaten, I'm certain. But I'm equally certain she wouldn't have touched Gloria; she never did.

Mrs McCrea came by once a week for the rent and my mother would chat away to her like an old friend. She also always made a point of paying what was due and getting Mrs McCrea to sign her rent book. That was deliberate, as I was to discover. When we'd been living there for a few weeks – it must have been about April, because it was getting warmer – Mrs McCrea asked my mother how her search for permanent accommodation was going: she was, after all, due to move out at the end of May. 'Oh, very well, thank you,' she answered. 'I'm just deciding which one to choose.' Mrs McCrea smiled – she was a nice woman – and went on her way. When she was out of earshot, my mother looked at Mac. 'Fucking stupid bitch,' she said. 'I've no intention of moving out. And she can't get me for being behind with the rent, either.' *Here we go again*, I thought, *More trouble brewing*.

The ridiculous thing was, as I later realised, that my mother would easily have qualified for being housed by the council. But she was much too snobbish for that. Only 'common people' – that's what she called them – lived in council houses. As it was, she was happy to sit it out in the caravan. But by the middle of May I could tell Mrs McCrea was getting anxious. She'd knock on the door and say, 'Pat, you are ready to move out soon, aren't you? I've got a booking for this caravan from the first of June.' And my mother would tell her not to worry.

There must have come a moment, though, when poor Morag McCrea guessed she'd been conned – she'd been good to my mother, and this was how she'd been repaid. She was probably going to lose the higher rent she'd have got from the holiday let, as well as having to return the deposit. But she also knew she'd get little sympathy from the other people on the caravan site if she tried to throw a mother and her five children on to the street. She couldn't win.

Mrs McCrea's worst fears were confirmed. When she came to collect the rent again, my mother handed over the money and told her we weren't moving. 'And you can't put me out with five kids. What are you going to look like?' Then she laughed in her face. After that, my mother made sure that there was always someone in the caravan. It was never to be left empty, she said, just in case Mrs McCrea was tempted to have it towed away.

I remember that day so clearly. It was the end of May and we had a week off school. We were sitting on the end of my mother's bed – Gezzie, me, Rob and Neil, all four of us with our feet dangling over the edge. Baby Penny was on the floor. My mother was there but Mac wasn't yet home; he was still working on the liners. There was a knock on the door: it was Mrs McCrea. She didn't want to argue with my mother, she said, but there were patches on the caravan's roof that needed repairing. Standing next to her was a handyman who'd come to do the work. Please would my mother let him get on with it?

'Oh, very well,' she replied in her la-di-da voice, as though she was doing everyone a terrific favour. I don't know who she thought she was kidding.

The man didn't need to come into the caravan, explained Mrs McCrea. So my mother shut the door and we all sat down to a tea of spam sandwiches. We could hear the man on the roof, making a bit of noise as he hammered away and unscrewed screws. We didn't take much notice of him until a small chink of daylight became visible above our heads. Slowly it got larger as first one foot and then the other appeared through the hole.

'Don't worry, Mrs McGinley,' said the handyman. 'This won't take long.' We couldn't believe what was happening. Before our very eyes, the roof of the caravan was being peeled back like a sardine tin. Within a very short time we were open to the sky.

My mother stormed out of the caravan to confront Mrs McCrea, who was still standing there. 'What the fuck's going on?' she demanded, quite forgetting her Lady Muck voice.

Mrs McCrea stood her ground. 'Pat,' she said, 'I'm not proud of what I've done. But what you've done to me is so rotten and filthy you've given me no choice. You tricked me. Now you're moving out.'

And then, as if by magic, the heavens opened. It bucketed down. People were hanging out of their caravans to watch what was happening and then two tarpaulins were rustled up from somewhere. 'Bad luck, love,' they said to my mother, and then started heckling poor Mrs McCrea. 'How could you do something like that?' they shouted.

As it turned out, one large tarpaulin would have been better. Where the two small ones met the rain quickly collected and started dripping into the middle of the caravan. My mother was screaming at us to fetch every saucepan and bowl to catch the water, and Gezzie and I were made to bale it out of the door before it overflowed from any of the pots. But the bedding and the carpeting had been drenched, and it took two days to dry everything out properly.

Little Penny developed such a bad chest that she was rushed into hospital the next day. She got so ill that it was touch and go at one stage, although she did then start responding to treatment. In the meantime, someone at the hospital must have phoned the council. My mother had told her sob story to the doctors and nurses and they'd said there was no way Penny would be allowed back to live in those conditions.

In a matter of days a three-bedroom council house with a toilet and fully fitted bathroom – the first I'd ever known – and a nice garden at the front and back was found at Mablethorpe Road, Wymering, about three miles from Suffolk Road. Gloria and I still had to share a bedroom, but even so there was much more room in the house than we had ever had before. There were the three bedrooms upstairs, plus another little room downstairs that could have been a bedroom although it was never converted. The bathroom was on the ground floor, as well as a sitting room and a kitchen. By this stage we had a television, which was in the sitting room. I liked watching any factual programmes, including the news, and any detective story.

For a month my mother was very taken with the novelty of it all, and I thought maybe we'd be all right now. I should have known better. Very quickly after that she reverted to her old ways, and if anything she was even worse. I might get home from school and she'd immediately ask me to make her some sandwiches. But she'd be sitting with her feet on the mantelpiece and a cigarette hanging out of her mouth. So I'd say to her, 'I've been at school all day. Couldn't you make your own sandwiches?' Then she'd pull herself to her feet, cross the room and slap me round my face. 'Don't you fucking answer me back, you little bastard!' she'd snap. 'Just get in the kitchen and do it.' And, when I'd done what she wanted I'd have to comb her hair for an hour or two, her feet back on the mantelpiece as she fell into a sort of trance.

Initially, of course, no one in Wymering knew my mother or her reputation. Not that it was long before the Cosham police force, as opposed to the Portsmouth one, came to know their new resident very well indeed. Back in a home of her own, and protected by brick walls that absorbed the noise, my mother was soon up to her old tricks. There were more rows on a more regular basis in that house than at any other time in my life. And she didn't have to be drunk to pick a fight, as I quickly found out. It was as if she was revelling in her release from the caravan where she'd been forced to rein in her temper – and, just as in the old times, I was the target. She went looking for trouble.

She had a habit, to take just one example, of opening her purse in front of us and counting out the coins over and over. 'I'm sure there was more in here,' she'd insist. What she was trying to suggest was that someone had stolen from her.

I'll never forget one of these incidents. We were in the kitchen and she started the old routine with the purse. 'I'm two shillings short,' she stated.

'What are you looking at me for?' I said. I wasn't a thief – she knew how much I hated anything to do with stealing.

'Well, it was there this morning,' she said. And then, luckily, she got distracted by something else.

But the next day she was in the kitchen again and suddenly called for Gezzie and me. We ran into the room. 'I was right,' she snapped. 'I'm not fucking stupid. You know the two shillings you said wasn't missing?' She was looking directly at me now.

'But I haven't touched your purse,' I protested.

'Oh, really?' she said disbelievingly. 'Then what are these two wrappers I found in the cupboard?' One was from a Wagon Wheel, the other from a Mars bar. 'They're empty. Someone's eaten them. That's where my fucking two shillings went.'

Gloria immediately piped up, 'Well, you know I wouldn't do something like that.'

Mother smiled at her. 'Don't worry, love,' she said, 'I know you wouldn't.' Then she wheeled round on me. 'It had to be you, didn't it?' she snarled, and with that she belted me all round the kitchen, her fists pounding down on my body as I tried in vain to protect myself. At one stage my head hit the back door so hard I thought I was going to pass out. But eventually she stopped and, thinking she'd lost interest, I staggered to my feet and headed for the door. Suddenly, however, my mother picked up a saucer from the draining board and came running at me. 'You ugly little bitch!' she screamed, and smashed it over my head with such force that it broke clean in two.

And Gloria, who I'm afraid I believe to this day was as guilty as hell, just sat and watched.

7

Counting the Days

By the time I reached my early teens in the mid-1950s, I felt only hatred and contempt for my mother. I'd been beaten so often and pummelled and mistreated and spoken to like filth, made to feel so ugly and utterly worthless, that I was beyond caring. It was a wonder that despite all this physical violence I didn't suffer any broken bones. But I was told by a doctor recently that my bones are big and strong. Just as well.

I believed then that my mother couldn't do any worse than she'd done already, and knew that one day in the not too distant future I'd be free of her for ever. In my last couple of years at school, whenever she threatened me with another belting I told her she could do what she wanted because it wouldn't be long before I'd be leaving home and never coming back. The kitchen in Mablethorpe Road wasn't very large, so it was hard to get away from her if she was in a vicious mood. She had a broom hanging from a hook on the wall. One of her favourite habits, if I'd said or done something to annoy her, was to reach out for the broom and then hit me across my back with the handle. I can still remember the searing pain. By that stage I was taller than her, and yet it never once occurred to me to hit her back. She went to her grave without my ever having laid a finger on her. I never descended to her level, and I'm proud of that.

Whenever and wherever possible I kept myself to myself, leaving Gloria and my mother to their cosy little chats. They seemed to be getting closer and closer – although that didn't mean my mother wasn't prepared to let Gezzie take the blame for something if it got *her* out of trouble. The infamous incident with Jack Lord demonstrated that. I was thirteen and we'd been living in Wymering for a couple of years. In those days it was quite the fashion for women to earn a bit of extra money by becoming house-to-house agents, either for large fashion or beauty catalogues or for enterprising individuals. This was the era of the Avon lady.

Jack Lord was someone my mother had known since before the war. He earned his living from buying supplies directly from warehouses – undies, stockings, socks, baby clothes, wool, knitting needles and so on – and using a network of housewives to sell to their friends and neighbours the contents of the cardboard box he gave them. Every so often he'd call round to see what supplies his agents needed to keep their boxes fully stocked. The agents paid Jack Lord for each item they'd sold and he gave them commission on every sale.

We were in the lounge in Mablethorpe Road one day when my mother saw a man get out of a car and knock on the door of one of the houses opposite. 'Good God!' she said. 'I think that's Jack Lord.' She went and called out to him, and in he came for a cup of tea and a chat. It didn't take her long to agree to become one of his agents. So he retrieved a large cardboard box of supplies from his car, she signed for it and he said he'd be back in a couple of weeks to see how she was getting on. Well, of course, she herself rarely went out selling – I think she managed it twice in six months – but she didn't have to: invariably she made me do it. I had to deliver the goods and collect the money on any sales, but she wouldn't allow me to keep any of it for myself. I didn't like going from house to house after dark, especially with money on me, but she was deaf to my anxieties.

One day my mother sat me down and explained her latest scam. Jack would be at our house in about an hour. When he came inside she'd offer him a cup of tea, draw the curtains – despite the fact that it would still be daylight – and they'd sit down for a chat. As soon as that happened I was to go out of the back door, down the side of the house – the brick entry, we called it, the covered alley that divided our house from our neighbour's – and remove one of the big cardboard boxes from Jack's shooting-brake. I was to bring it indoors as quickly as possible and take it straight upstairs. 'He doesn't lock his car,' she said, 'so it won't be a problem.'

I looked at her. 'I will not,' I objected. 'I'm not stealing for you or anyone else.'

I thought she was going to hit me. 'Well, fuck you!' she retorted in disgust. 'Gloria, will you do it?' And Gezzie said she would.

When Jack arrived, my mother was all over him. 'Oh, how lovely to see you,' she cooed, then addressed me in unfamiliar terms: 'Pat, love, go and put the kettle on, will you?' And with that she pulled the curtains.

In the kitchen, I begged Gloria not to go ahead with our mother's plan. But she wouldn't listen. Within minutes she was back inside, carrying a box almost bigger than herself and containing all sorts which, quickly and quietly, she took up the stairs and into my mother's bedroom.

As soon as she'd said goodbye to Jack my mother was straight upstairs to see what Gloria had stolen. She was still rifling through the box when there was a knock at the front door and she went downstairs. Jack was standing there, looking crestfallen. 'You're not going to believe this, Pat,' he said, 'but while I've been talking to you someone's been into my car and stolen a box of supplies.'

She looked at him with a horrified expression. 'Never!' she exclaimed. I didn't know where to put myself and could feel my face turning bright red. My mother asked Jack what he was going to do. He couldn't let it pass, he said; he'd have to report it to the police. And then he was gone.

'He knows nothing,' my mother said coolly to us once he was out of earshot. 'We'll be fine.' Half an hour later we watched as his car drove up the road again. He got out, but didn't come straight to our front door. When we looked again we could see him talking to our next-door neighbour, Mrs Butcher, a tough, working-class woman with nine kids she was bringing up on her own after her man had put his head in the gas oven. She despised my mother for her phoney snobbish ways. 'Don't you look down on me,' Mrs Butcher would shout over the garden fence. 'I may not have been married to my man – but you aren't married to Mac. So you can stop that rubbish.' And my mother would stick her nose in the air. 'Oh, you're a very common woman,' she'd say in her pretend-posh accent. There was certainly no love lost there.

It turned out that when Jack had returned from the police station Mrs Butcher had walked down the grass verge in front of her house to meet him. 'You looking for your box?' she'd said. 'Gloria took it. I watched her out of my front window – she went to your car, took the box out of the boot and then went back in through the brick entry. I saw her do it.' Jack thanked her – Mrs Butcher was only too pleased to have got one over on my mother – and marched over to our front door. My mother opened it, all innocence. 'I'm sorry to tell you this,' said Jack, 'but your daughter, the elder one with the ginger hair, has stolen my box.'

My mother put a hand to her heart before shouting up the stairs, 'Gloria, get down here at once!' When my sister appeared, she asked her, 'Gloria, did you steal a box from the car of Jack Lord, my dear friend of many years' standing?' My God, she really should have been on the stage! Gloria meekly nodded her head and admitted the theft. 'Well, fetch that box here immediately,' commanded my mother, full of mock outrage.

Jack looked at her. 'I'm sorry, Pat,' he said. 'If I'd have known it was your daughter I'd never have reported it to the police. You and I have been friends for a long time. But I've got no choice now. I'll have to tell them who stole the box.'

Even so, when the police turned up about an

hour later he asked if there was any way they could turn a blind eye to what had happened. But one of the bobbies explained that since the crime had been reported they had to follow it up. Jack went off with them to make his statement, but not before my mother was told to bring Gloria down to the police station in an hour so she could be interviewed.

I knew that was never going to happen, and I was right. As soon as they were out of the door my mother turned to me. 'I'm not going to any police station,' she said. 'You can go with her. You can keep her company. But don't you dare open your fucking mouth.'

So Gezzie and I walked down the hill to Cosham police station and she was charged with stealing. To this day, I don't know why she played along with all of this. But, for some reason I never understood, my mother knew she would cover for her. I said to her, 'Gezzie, you know our mother put you up to this. How can you let her get away with it?' She wasn't interested; even in the police station, under cross-examination, she never turned a hair. No matter how badly our mother behaved, Gloria would always stick up for her. They had an unspoken closeness, and were – quite literally, in the circumstances – as thick as thieves. You wouldn't have caught me reacting like that. I always knew my mother was a rotter and I wasn't ever going to let her get away with pinning things on me, even if it meant more or less constant abuse.

When we got home, the first words out of my mother's mouth were, 'You didn't mention me, did you?' We told her we hadn't, but she never thanked either of us. Are you kidding? It did mean, though, that she was in Gloria's debt for some time and in mine, too; and she knew it. She calmed down for a few months. Not that it stopped Gloria having to go to court, where she was put on probation for three years. I went with her but – surprise, surprise – my mother didn't show her face.

My sister's probation officer was a rather strange woman called Miss De Hammill. Gezzie had to report to her once a week and Miss De Hammill would visit my mother from time to time to find out how her charge was getting on. My mother would assure her that she was keeping a very careful eye on her wayward daughter. Oh, the hypocrisy of it all! I didn't know how but I vowed to tell the truth one day about the whole business of my mother and Gezzie and Jack Lord's missing box.

It can't have been long after this that my father turned up at the door one day. I couldn't have been more surprised – I hadn't seen him in years. Standing next to him was a young woman called Betty who was only eight years older than me, as it turned out. He introduced her to my mother as his girlfriend. He'd met her, he explained, when he was stationed in Liverpool, her home city, where she'd worked in a bar popular with servicemen. She was now his fiancée, he added.

I could see my mother's eyes narrowing. 'Yes?' she enquired.

Without further ado he asked my mother, bold as brass and with Betty right beside him, whether she'd remarry him. What's more, he said he'd take Mac's kids on.

My mother looked at him. I held my breath. This was something she'd wanted to hear for so many years, and I honestly thought she might say yes. But she didn't. 'Are you mad?' she said. 'I've got all these kids with Mac. I can't marry you.'

'In that case,' he replied, 'if *you* won't marry me I'll marry Betty.'

To this day I haven't a clue what he was up to, but Betty just seemed to accept it all and never opened her mouth. Then they were off. A few months later, he sent a letter to the house. 'Well, girls,' it read, 'Betty and I are married.' Perhaps he was trying to twist the knife into my mother. I'll never know the truth of it. It was a mystery that Gezzie and I never unravelled, and how Betty could have borne it beggars belief.

When I went to live with him and Betty a few

years later, I asked my father why he'd behaved in the way he had. He denied it. I told him that I'd been there, that with my own ears I'd heard him offer to remarry my mother. 'It never happened,' he said. And I was very surprised by my mother's reaction – I'd have thought that what my father had asked her was just what she wanted. But although she was rowing with Mac daily at that time, she'd known enough to refuse his offer. He seemed to be playing with her, and I think she'd worked that out. Then again, there had always been something between those two. I remembered the day my father had turned up with the bicycles for my sister and me and a toy crocodile for Rob. He'd told Gezzie and me to stay out for an hour to get used to our bikes, and Rob was sent to play with a boy who lived opposite. Although it's impossible to say for sure, I'm pretty much convinced now that my parents were having a physical relationship while we kids were out of the way and Mac was at work. The attraction between them lasted years after the marriage was effectively over. What a family! None of it made any sense then, and none of it makes any sense now.

While living at Mablethorpe Road I attended the secondary modern school in Wymering, but as a newcomer I didn't know any of the other girls and I didn't want to be there. The only subject I enjoyed was English. Arithmetic tied me in knots;

even today I couldn't tell you what a fraction or a decimal point is, or what they're for. And I hated physical education. Miss Parker, the PE teacher, had dark hair and bony knees. She'd put her hands on her hips and complain to me, 'Pat McKenzie, I'm sick, tired and *weary* of you and your excuses.' She always said the same thing, always shouted the word 'weary' and always ended up with: 'You'll do as I tell you.' But I wouldn't, because I couldn't. Just because I was tall, it was assumed I'd be good at the high jump or running or climbing ropes. But I wasn't. And, of course, my eyesight was very poor – although I didn't yet known it – and I didn't have any glasses.

I was a teenager by now, but skinny and flat-chested with buck teeth that made me look like Brer Rabbit. My Uncle Neville used to tease me. When I watched him playing football in Bransbury Park he'd call out to me, 'Hello, Pat. Are you a 36 double D cup yet?' He wasn't being mean – it was said out of affection – but it made me feel embarrassed. Sometimes, when I walked past, some of the other kids would sing a popular song of the day:

> I know a girl called Bony Maroney
> She's got a figure like a stick of macaroni

Early teens can be a difficult time, whether you're male or female, but I think I must have appeared particularly awkward. My strange home life, my height and my lack of social skills combined to make me an outsider. I'd learnt from such an early age to be a survivor against the odds that I'd become someone who didn't need – and certainly didn't seek out – other people. A combination of loner and rebel, at school – I must have seemed something of an outcast; I certainly felt it. In truth I don't think there was much wrong with the school, but I was never in the right frame of mind for it. I was always worried about what would be waiting for me when I got home. There'd be housework to do – ironing, cleaning, washing the younger kids' clothes and so on. When I'd finished, I'd escape and go walking up on the hills behind the house, occasionally with a girl from school called Vera, but usually on my own. I preferred my own company.

My mind was always full of plans for getting away. There was a girl called Josephine Mayle, whom I'd sometimes hang around with after school. I told her I wanted to go to America and become a film star, but that I didn't dare go alone. Would she come with me? I was a funny mixture of confidence, in that I felt I could look after myself, and deep-seated anxiety. I suffered from agoraphobia; to an extent, I still do. I didn't mind being by myself on the Wymering hills because I could see my house. But, although I'm a loner, I still don't like being in unfamiliar circumstances on my own. And yet I can happily stand up and talk to an invited audience and really enjoy the experience.

Trapped in Mablethorpe Road, I couldn't wait to be an adult even though I was still very naïve, in many ways. I didn't start going through puberty until I was fourteen and a half, which was very late; Gezzie had begun at eleven. One day I was walking home after school and suddenly noticed blood running down my leg. When I got home, I told my mother that I thought I was having my first period.

'Oh, so you've become a woman, have you?' she commented, and that was it. She never explained the details of what was happening to me, or why. She never comforted me, or asked if there were any questions I needed to ask her.

I knew there were sanitary towels in the bathroom cupboard because Gezzie had told me. As usual, I just got on with things on my own.

I was fifteen on 25 March 1957 and left school just a few days later, at the end of the Easter term. In my mind I'd been ticking off the days to my longed for freedom. The last teacher I saw was Miss Bishop, who used to take us for needlepoint. I'd been restless all day, quite mischievous for me, because I knew it was only a matter of hours before I'd be finished with school for ever. But I wanted to say goodbye to Miss Bishop, and anyway she had to give me my end-of-school report. When I found her, though, she said I couldn't have it because I'd been naughty. I could have waited until she handed it over – and I knew she would have done – but I couldn't be bothered. I was ill-educated, and I didn't need a report to tell me that. I also knew that my mother would never ask to see it: she couldn't have cared one way or the other.

I may have been free of school but the law said you couldn't leave home until you were sixteen. My father had legal custody of me, but most of the time he wasn't in Portsmouth because he was still serving in the Marines. So I was trapped with my mother for another year, and she was now worse than ever: because she was drinking from the moment she got up. The atmosphere grew so distressing that my nerves started to suffer and my hair began to fall out: I'd wake up in the morning and find small clumps of it on the pillow. I knew I had to get away as soon as possible for my own sanity.

I knew money would help, so I looked for a job. It didn't take long before I found one in a fashion shop in North End, where I had to iron the dresses for the window-dresser, make the tea and take the post to the post office: I was in fact a general dogsbody earning two pounds a week, all of which I had to give to my mother except for the bus fare. So much for trying to save up to help me gain my freedom. The shop-floor assistants were much older than me and very bossy, constantly ordering me to carry this and fetch that. After a lifetime of that at home, it was the last thing I needed at work. In the event I only lasted there a couple of months, but my mother insisted I didn't leave until I'd found something else. Not that she was interested in my welfare – it was my wage packet she wanted.

Then I saw an advert in the window of a record shop just up the road from where I was working; they were looking for an assistant, and I was quickly offered the job. At least I'd now have direct contact with the public and not be stuck in some back room. But I soon realised my lot hadn't really improved. Putting records back in their right slot was hardly a dream job, and I was still run down and depressed which had physical effects too. My hair continued to fall out and people were starting to comment; added to which, at an especially sensitive time as I grew into a young woman, I was suffering from bad acne. I was bending down one day to put some records on a lower shelf when I overheard two of the other assistants talking. 'Look at her,' said one of them. 'She's going bald. And have you seen the spots on her face?' I wanted to cry and run out of the shop there and then. The only solution, or so I reasoned, was yet again to change jobs. I got taken on at Woolworth's just down the road – I was on the pet supplies counter – and stayed there, perfectly happily, for a few months. It was busy and the people were nice. Anyway, anything was better than being at home.

When Gezzie left school, my mother had taken her to the shops and bought her a three-piece suit – a jacket and two skirts, one pencil, one pleated – new shoes, new handbag, new blouse, new stockings. She chose to stay at home, though, and help with the younger children. When it came to my turn, I got the cheapest suit my mother could find in a catalogue plus a pair of shoes, and I had to order both items myself. It was obvious that she couldn't summon up any interest in me.

Throughout it all I never confided in Gezzie about my plans to escape because I knew anything I said risked being repeated to my mother. But what I couldn't work out was how I'd be able to leave home without any savings. And then a piece of pure good fortune fell into my lap. Around Christmas 1957, just three months before my sixteenth birthday, my mother said out of the blue one day that my father's final posting before being demobbed was going to be back in Portsmouth. He and Betty and their small daughter, Jean, were going to live in an Admiralty house in Copnor, near my Aunty Terry, and then they were planning to move up to Betty's home town of Liverpool.

My mother had plans, too. She said she needed more money – I expect she was behind with the rent again – and for that reason we were going to visit my father. After I turned sixteen she'd only be getting the Admiralty allowance for Rob, and now would be a good time to get that increased.

I looked at her. 'Why should he give you more money?' I asked.

But instead of hitting me, she smiled. 'He will,' she said. 'Otherwise I'll dump Robert on him.'

It was snowing as Gloria, Rob and I set out with our mother to my father's final Admiralty house. She wouldn't go on public transport, which she considered was for people far inferior to her. Instead she ordered a taxi and told the driver to set us down a few doors from my dad's place. She paid the man, then turned to the three of us. 'Right,' she said, 'I want you lot to pick up a handful of snow and rub it into your hair. We're going to pretend we've walked from Wymering.'

We did as we were told – we could see she meant business – and then she knocked on the door.

My father opened it and his face fell. 'Oh, Christ,' he groaned, 'what do you want now?'

She said, 'Ron, I haven't had any money off Mac for a few weeks. He's buggered off.' This was a complete lie. Mac was at home and working full-time. 'We've walked all the way from Wymering. We're frozen to the marrow.'

What could my father do? He had no choice but to let us in out of the cold.

Then she started on her carefully rehearsed sob story. She told him she couldn't manage without more money from him to pay for Rob, who may not have been his natural son but was, as she reminded him, his legal responsibility. She wasn't getting any Admiralty allowance for Gloria, who was now seventeen; and my sixteenth birthday was just around the corner. Oh, she didn't know where to turn.

I'm sure my father knew he was being spun a line, but he wanted her out of there. So he gave her a few pounds before we left his house, walked up the road to a minicab rank and took a taxi home.

I may not have learned much at school, but you don't survive for more than fifteen years in what felt more like a war zone than a home without getting canny. That little episode had shown me where my father lived. I'd also been told that he'd have to give up that house in early March when he was demobbed. I was within weeks of my sixteenth birthday. I knew my father wouldn't want me back in his life on a permanent basis, but if I could somehow persuade him to pay for me to go to Liverpool with him when he, Betty and little Jean moved there I'd be free of my mother for good. I'd also worked out that there was very little risk she'd come after me; she rarely went out of the house as it was. She'd never been back to Sunderland, for instance, to reclaim Richard, so why would she bother coming up to Liverpool for a daughter she openly despised? Anyway, I'd be sixteen soon enough and then she couldn't touch me.

There was no doubt that my father was heading north. Betty's brother, Eddie, had recently died in a motorbike accident and she was the only other child. She was keen to go and stay with her mum and dad in Liverpool and comfort them, and my father didn't mind where he lived. He hoped to get a brewery to take him on as licensee of a pub, something that a lot of ex-servicemen did. And, although new surroundings frightened me, anywhere on God's earth was better than living with my mother. I wasn't yet sure quite how I was going to achieve it, but I was absolutely determined I was going to Liverpool, too.

Christmas 1957 came and went with the usual rows and screaming matches between my mother and Mac. A new trick of hers was to run up the hill at the back of our house, then sit on the edge of the huge chalk pit at the top and threaten to throw herself off. Of course, she never did. On one occasion, she took a hot water bottle up there with her, which made me laugh – it didn't look to me as though she was about to end it all! As it turned out, she came back indoors when it got cold. She pulled this stunt on numerous occasions, and each time, when she realised that no one was taking any notice of her – in fact, when she worked out that we were all glad to see the back of her and were finally enjoying a bit of peace and quiet and the neighbours were laughing about her behind their twitching curtains – she'd return to the house, causing yet more trouble as she fell into another bottle of her precious VP port wine. Wherever possible, I tried to avoid her. I was out at work every day anyway and I was giving her money so, although I'd still get hit if the mood took her and I didn't duck in time, it wasn't so often or so severe.

Until Valentine's Day, that is.

8

Hit and Run

The fourteenth of February 1958, is a day I'll never forget for as long as I live.

It was a bitingly cold night as I arrived home in Mablethorpe Road after another day's work at Woolworth's. About an hour or so later, Mac appeared. But he did something he'd never done before: he brought home two male friends who worked alongside him painting the liners in Southampton Docks. He explained that they lived near us and they'd given him a lift home because the weather was so bad. He couldn't possibly have cycled home in those conditions. By way of saying thank you, he'd invited them in for a drink. Rob and Neil were upstairs, playing in their bedroom, while my mother, Gezzie and I were in the lounge with the two little ones, Penny and baby Rosemary, who'd been born the previous year. Mac went off to fetch a few bottles of beer from the kitchen, then gave my mother another glass of VP port wine. She wasn't drunk but she was on the way. One of the men asked her what my name was, and she told him I was called Pat.

'Well, I'll tell you something,' he said, giving me an admiring glance. 'When that girl becomes a woman, she's going to be very good-looking.'

My mother eyed him. 'Do you think so?' she said sceptically.

'Oh, she's a nice-looking girl *now*,' he said. He turned to me. 'But you wait till you blossom, love. You're going to break a few hearts.' The other man nodded his head in agreement.

I could see this hadn't gone down too well with my mother and to this day I don't know what got into me, but I suddenly said, 'It's funny you should say that, because all my life my mother's told me I'm an ugly little cow.'

She looked at me as though she could kill me. 'No, I haven't,' she said, filling an awkward silence.

I wasn't in the mood for backing down, though. 'Yes, you have,' I said, 'and you know it.'

For a split second it was as if the earth had stopped turning. And then my mother erupted. 'You want to try fucking living with her!' she snarled.

Mac was on his feet immediately, trying to shut her up. He'd seen her like this too many times before. 'No, come on, Pat . . .' he began.

'And don't you fucking start,' she snapped. 'Anyway, who asked you to bring home these fucking arseholes?'

The two men exchanged glances, and I could tell they thought they'd walked into a madhouse. My mother carried on effing and blinding as the two men stood up. One of them said he thought it was better if they left, and then they were out of that house like greased lightning.

No sooner was the front door closed than my mother started to hit me on any part of my body where she could land a punch or a slap. She knocked me the length and breadth of the living room as I cried and pleaded with her. 'Don't blame me,' I sobbed, and then I turned to Mac. 'You shouldn't be bringing your friends home. I can't help what they say.' And that did it. All the tension that had been bottled up in him boiled over. He'd been made to look silly in front of his workmates, and no one likes to be humiliated. I think he just snapped.

Mac just strode across the room and threw me at the window – it's a wonder I didn't go through it. Then he got me against the wall and started thumping hell out of me, totally out of control. He punched me as hard as he could all over my body, apparently unable to stop. It was one of the worst beatings of my life. I was trying to shield myself with my arms, but he was raining blows down on me anywhere he could reach and he was a strong man. Although I was screaming for him to stop he just kept pounding away. Was he going to kill me?

Just as he took another swing of his arm to wallop me again I somehow managed to duck and run past him through the hall and out of the front door. And I just kept on running. I was wearing a cardigan and skirt, stockings and shoes but no coat. I'd dyed my white undies black because they were getting old and I thought it would make them look fresher. The freezing cold rain was pouring down, and within minutes the dye was leaking through and staining all my clothes a dirty grey. But I didn't care.

I ran to the corner of the road where a bus was waiting. I knew, if I could reach it in time, that it would take me to Copnor where I could throw myself on my father's mercy. As it started off, I jumped on board. The shocked bus conductor took one look at me and said, 'What's up, love?' I was coughing and choking and crying but managed to stammer that I didn't have any money. He said, 'Go on, you're all right. We'll take you to where you want to go.' I found a seat, ignoring the stares of the other passengers, and sat there huddled in a little ball, soaking wet, frozen and in pain all over, until we got to Copnor Bridge about fifteen minutes later.

My father's house was at the end of a long road. As soon as I was off the bus I ran like the wind, looking over my shoulder all the time, just in case my mother was behind me. She couldn't have been, of course, but not surprisingly I wasn't thinking straight. Then I tripped and fell and cut my knee. But what was one more injury to my bruised and battered body? I picked myself up quickly. My chest was aching with the cold and the running but I wouldn't stop. I daren't.

When I got to my father's house I banged on the door with my fists. He opened it and took one look at me.

'God almighty, Little Pat,' he said in horror. 'What on earth's happened to you?' He told Betty to get me a cup of tea as he pulled me inside to get warm by the fire. 'She's frozen through,' he said.

When I got my breath back I managed to blurt out my story about Mac's workmates and what one of them had said about me and how that had led to an almighty row and being beaten almost senseless by both my mother and Mac. 'I'm not going back,' I said. 'I'm never going back. Will you take me to Liverpool with you? Please.' I was pleading with him, and deep down I knew he didn't want to look bad in front of Betty.

'Of course,' he said, and that's when I started crying again. I didn't know what the future held, but it had to be better than this. Or so I thought.

Betty made a nice meal for me and gave me some dry clothes. She said she'd go out shopping for me the next day and buy me some new undies. Then they made up a bed for me on the floor of the lounge and, exhausted and aching all over, I sank into a deep sleep. I was free of that terrible woman. In three weeks' time I was off up north. I was on my way.

Nevertheless I could tell from my father's attitude over the next few days that me turning up like that on his doorstep wasn't exactly the best thing that had ever happened to him. But he was nice enough to me. In my heart I knew he didn't love me, but I'd had enough time to get used to that. I also knew he wouldn't take me back to my mother's. In their continuing battle with each other, this was a small and rare victory for him. I'd run away from her to be with him.

For once in my life, luck had smiled on me. I couldn't help feeling that Portsmouth being my father's last posting, just as I was turning sixteen, was meant to be. It had given me my escape route. Now, I had a warm roof over my head. I wasn't going to be beaten again. I'd get to Liverpool and find a job. If it didn't work out with my father, I'd have the money to rent a little bedsit. I was at peace for the first time in my life. And almost immediately my hair started growing back.

Two days later there was a knock on the door. Betty came into the lounge, where I was sitting. 'It's the Queer One,' she said. She always referred to my mother as the Queer One. I could hear my mother demanding to see me and my father telling her she couldn't. I was sure he wouldn't hand me over, but that didn't stop my whole body from shaking. I knew why she was here and it wasn't because she loved me. Both the family and the Admiralty allowance for me may have been about to run out, but I was useful to her for the money I brought home from my job. And then there was her pride. She couldn't bear my father having one over on her.

They continued to argue back and forth in the hall until I heard my father say that the only way he'd let my mother see me was if I agreed. 'I'll go and ask her,' he said. The knowledge that he had control of the situation must have killed her, and I just knew he was enjoying having the upper hand. When he came into the lounge I told him I never wanted to speak to her again.

His response surprised me. 'Best to see what she wants,' he advised. 'But if she starts any trouble, Betty and I will be in the kitchen.'

So, reluctantly, I agreed. He went to fetch her and led her into the room.

'I want to see her on her own,' announced my mother.

'All right,' said my father, 'but no nonsense now.' Then off he went into the kitchen with Betty.

Oh, it was a joy! I looked at my mother. Her hair, nails and make-up were perfect, as ever; I could smell Evening in Paris as she walked in. She was nobody's fool. She didn't come in all guns blazing, but was bright enough to know that she had to tread carefully. However much she resented it I was living quite legitimately in my father's house; he was my legal guardian, as she well knew. Indeed, I only had another month to go before I could do whatever I wanted. She had one more month's family allowance for me, as well as the potential of my weekly pay packet. The chips were down.

I was on strong ground and I knew it. Even so, my heart was hammering in my chest. I was certain my father wouldn't let me down: he was both keen to play the good guy in front of Betty while savouring every moment of holding the trump card, for once in his life, over my mother. I knew I had her: there was nothing she could do or say that would make me go back with her to Mablethorpe Road. For the first time in my life, she couldn't make me do something against my will and she wouldn't dare knock me about.

But that still didn't stop me feeling nervous. 'What do you want?' I asked, trying to keep the anxiety out of my voice.

'I want you to come back home,' she replied.

I looked her in the eye. 'In that case,' I said, 'you must be mad.' The words came spilling out. 'You wicked, evil old bag! I'm ashamed to call you my mother. I've hated you for so long I can't put my hatred into words.'

She looked at me, eyes all wide. 'What have I ever done to you?' she said.

I was amazed. 'I'll tell you what you've done. You've beaten me with your fists and hurt me so much with your cruel words almost since the day I was born. And all because I wasn't a boy. Mac's beaten me, too. Just look at these bruises.' And I showed her some of the purple and black marks on my body. 'I've dreamt of this moment for so long and now you can't touch me any more. It's over. The end. Now get out!'

My mother knew the game was up. There was no shouting; there were no histrionics. My overwhelming feeling was one of utter relief. At last I'd been able to say what I truly felt without any risk of brutal retaliation. And that felt good.

Having heard my raised voice, my father

appeared from the kitchen. 'I think you'd better leave,' he said to my mother.

And she did. She turned on her heel and walked out of the room, out of the house, out of my life. It was another forty years and more before she died and I only ever saw her alive once more – and that was once too many.

My father was to be demobbed on 6 March 1958, his birthday, and then we were off to Liverpool to stay with Betty's mum and dad until my father found a job as a publican. If he was successful, it would also give us somewhere to live. But there was one piece of unfinished business I was determined to complete before I left Portsmouth for good. I had to go and see Gloria's probation officer and set the record straight.

Sitting in Miss De Hammill's office I told her the true story of the theft of Jack Lord's box. She listened in silence, and when I'd finished she simply said, 'You know, it's a funny thing. Despite everything she said, I had a feeling your mother was part and parcel of all that.' But she explained that, since the case had come to court and Gloria had been placed on probation for three years, there was no way in law that the file could be reopened. I don't know if my mother ever found out that I'd revealed her involvement in the crime. It was years before I mentioned to Gezzie what I'd done, and I've no idea if she passed the information on. I rather doubt it. But that wasn't the point. It was a wrong that needed righting. Now I was free to go to Liverpool and start my new life.

9

Out in the World

As soon as you stepped inside Betty's parents' house in Liverpool, you could sense the sadness. The mother was a small Welsh woman who wore her hair in a tight bun and busied herself round the house to take her mind off their recent bereavement. But the father wasn't coping at all. He'd sit in his chair in the living room and cry and cry, which was awful to see.

It wasn't a big house. My father and Betty slept in one room, with little Jean in a cot beside them. Betty's parents were in another. And I had their dead son's old room. But I couldn't sleep. It was a tiny little box room with a single bed, and all round the walls Eddie's clothes were hanging on hooks: his shirts, his suits, his motorbike gloves, his crash helmet. His watch lay on the bedside table. Eddie's parents had moved nothing, and turned his room into a shrine. I was terrified and next morning went to my dad in tears, telling him I couldn't spend another night there. I was sure he'd tell me not to be so silly but, thoughtfully, he moved the double bed into Eddie's room and I slept in what had been his and Betty's room.

My father had written to a number of breweries before we got to Liverpool, and had been offered some interviews as a result. He'd been awarded the British Empire Medal (BEM) and I think that went down well. My mother always used to say it should have been BUM. She wrote to him once and addressed the envelope 'Ronald McKenzie BUM', but he didn't care. He was proud of his medal. While my father went to his interviews I got myself a job in Woolworth's in a district of Liverpool called Old Swan. I was put on the personal toiletries counter. I've always been a bit embarrassed about bodily functions and I didn't like having to sell sanitary products, but the atmosphere in the shop was good and I made two friends: Little Mo and Barbara Cutts. I was there a few months, and then my father hit the jackpot.

The Horse and Jockey was a lovely country pub in a picturesque village called Upton, on the Birkenhead side of the river Mersey. There was one room reserved exclusively for men with their pints and their pipes; a snug for the posh people, the gentlemen farmers with leather elbows on their tweed jackets; and a couples' room for cooing and doving. There was also a big family room, plus a dartboard in the main bar and illegal dominoes in the back; in those days you weren't supposed to play games for money, even if it was only pennies, but everybody did it. It was a classy little pub and he was lucky to get it. And there was lots of room upstairs for the resident manager and his family; in fact there was a whole floor at the top which we never used. The first floor, which we did use, had a big kitchen, a lounge and three bedrooms. There was no rent to pay, no rates, no telephone bills; the only thing Dad had to buy was the food we ate.

It was too far for me to commute to Woolworth's, so I started looking locally for another job. To begin with I was at home most of the day, and I can't say the atmosphere was good. Betty tried her best but, although she never showed it, I'm sure she would have preferred me not to be there. She had a husband with a demanding job, and a small child too. She didn't need a stepdaughter hanging around, and she had no idea how long I was going to stay. But then nor did I and I had nowhere else to go. Betty would cook for all of us every day and I'd sit there at mealtimes, a big, lumpy girl with little or nothing to say to my father. I felt awkward – hardly surprising, as I barely knew the man. When he lived with my mother in Portsmouth I was too young to remember him, and he'd been in the Marines, mostly stationed abroad, for most of my life. I'd only ever seen him a handful of times.

It was a strange time. Yes, the brutality had stopped. But I felt very isolated: I didn't know anyone, and I was living in unfamiliar surroundings amongst people whose accent I could hardly understand. I felt lonelier than ever. And at sixteen I was still a child, much younger for my age than a street-smart sixteen-year-old today. At school just one girl had fallen pregnant. She was fourteen, it caused the most almighty scandal, and she was sent away to live with an aunt as her pregnancy progressed. I didn't admit it out loud at the time, but I didn't really understand how she could be pregnant in the first place. Someone said they'd seen her with a boy and he was kissing her, his body pressed right up against hers. In my ignorance, I told myself that perhaps he'd got too close to her.

I could tell that Betty wasn't all that happy, either. Her life wasn't awful but it wasn't what she'd had in mind. Then, one day, I walked into the kitchen and innocently asked her what we were having for dinner. Without warning, she suddenly exploded. 'Oh, get out! Just get out!' she shouted. It was all becoming too much for her.

I said, 'What have I done, Betty?'

She was crying now. 'Please,' she sobbed, 'just leave me alone.'

I may have been naïve, but I think I understood her frustration. Later on, my father had a quiet word with me. He said that Betty didn't dislike me, but it would be for the best if I looked for a job where I could live in. There was no pressure – I could take my time. But Betty needed her own space.

Little wonder that my father wasn't forcing the issue. If Betty had known how he'd been behaving towards me, there would have been an almighty row. It was her habit to go into the village just after nine each morning to buy the fresh food she was going to cook that day. Almost as soon as she'd gone, my father would be at my bedroom door. 'Come on now,' he'd say. 'Time to get up.' He'd walk across to my bed, wrap his arms around my body until his hands met at the back, and then pull me up towards him so that I'd be touching his chest, his hot breath on my face.

I wore a bra and slip to sleep in; he was fully dressed in his white shirt and flannels. But I didn't like it. It felt wrong to me. I'd say, 'Leave me alone', and then I'd tell him I'd get up if he left the room. This went on morning after morning, and I hated it more than I can say. I explained that he could shout to me from the door; there was no need for him to come into the room. But he took no notice. Then one morning he sat on the bed, pulled me towards him and kissed me on my neck.

'Stop it!' I said. 'I'll tell Betty.'

Immediately he stood up and walked out of my bedroom. He and Betty had a good marriage and I wasn't about to rock that boat – I didn't want to hurt Betty, but my father knew the game was up. It worked. The morning visits to my bedroom stopped.

But there was worse to come: it will be imprinted on my mind for ever. Betty was wearing a pale green trenchcoat with a matching beret she'd just bought, and I told her how nice she looked as she went off to the village to buy that day's food. My father was down in the bar pulling the pumps through, so I went downstairs and asked him if he'd like a cup of tea.

He said, 'I'll come up for one shortly.' Then he looked at me and beckoned me over.

'What do you want?' I asked.

He said he had something he wanted to tell me. As I walked behind the bar, he said, 'Come on, don't be shy. Open your legs and let's have a feel.'

I couldn't believe what I was hearing. 'You dirty, filthy pig!' I screamed, and ran straight upstairs.

He didn't follow, and when Betty got back from the shops he couldn't have been more friendly and attentive to her. I could see he was scared I'd say something – although I had no intention of telling her anything. But I also knew I had to get out of there as soon as possible.

It didn't take me too long to come up with the solution. I'd been working briefly at Woolworth's in Moreton Cross, a short journey from the pub. But then I spotted an advert in the *Liverpool Echo* for a live-in cleaner in a large family house in Prenton, a well-heeled area about twenty minutes by bus from the pub. So I went for an interview with Mrs Hislop, a well-educated woman with a fancy accent who was married to a rather Victorian-looking man with a big moustache. He owned the first two launderettes to be opened in Birkenhead. The Hislops had two sons, Peter and his younger brother, Anthony, whom I'd be expected to collect from his preparatory school each weekday afternoon.

I don't know which of us was more relieved when I told my father I'd found a live-in job not far away. I knew I might feel lonely, but after the chaotic, abusive life I'd known up to that point I was willing to endure loneliness in order to get some peace and quiet. And my father was obviously pleased: with me gone Betty could relax again, while he wouldn't have to live with the possibility that I might reveal the sexual advances he'd made to me.

Mrs Hislop gave me a clean, tidy room with a nice bed, a grey carpet, a wardrobe in one corner and a basin in the other. But there was no television or radio. I was to be responsible for all the washing-up and cleaning, as well as polishing the silver and the brassware, while Mrs Hislop did all the cooking. Once a week, Mr Hislop would take the family's dirty clothes in two big bags to one of the launderettes he owned and then bring them home clean for me to spend a full day ironing them. There was no question of him including my clothes in the launderette wash – I was just the hired help. I'd rinse my things in the basin in my bedroom and then leave them to dry on the radiator.

On weekday evenings Mrs Hislop would prepare the family meal which I was allowed to eat, too – but not in the dining room with them. I had to eat in the little back sitting room. She brought my food out to me and then, when it was time for dessert, she'd ring a little bell she kept in the dining room and I'd go in and be handed my portion from the sideboard. 'Thenk you, Pet,' she'd say – that was how it sounded in her posh accent. 'I'll ring again when we've finished.' And I'd have to wait for the bell before I could go back in and start clearing the table after serving them their coffee in the sitting room.

Like anyone who doesn't have to worry about the mess they're making, Mrs Hislop always seemed to use every pot and pan in the place when she was preparing the evening meal. By the end, I had dishes up the wall to wash and dry and put away; and, of course, there were no dishwashers in those days. It would be quite late by the time I finished. I'd go and have a bath – I had my own little bathroom – and get ready for bed. I'd then wash out my undies in the basin with a bar of soap and perhaps read a magazine before putting the lights out. I longed for some company my own age. I was still only sixteen and for obvious reasons I didn't even feel I had a family I could turn to. I did ring my father to give him my new address, but he never got in touch.

The weekends were a bit more fun, though. Every Friday night, Mr and Mrs Hislop would go to the Bowler Hat, a smart club in Birkenhead. She'd get dressed up in a lovely gown and I'd be left babysitting the boys. But what I really looked forward to was being allowed to use the lounge and watch the big telly. I'd sit in front of it all evening, devouring anything and everything on screen. On Saturday, the Hislops would go out for dinner with friends. Again, I had all the TV entertainment I wanted.

I had one day off a week, on Sundays. I was paid two pounds ten shillings a week which wasn't a fortune by any means, but I had precious little to spend it on so it did mean I could start saving. I had a habit of taking the rugs outside to beat them, and that's how I got to know a girl called Pauline who worked as a live-in cleaner in the house opposite. She was a lovely girl, a Liverpudlian who like me had had a difficult childhood. Sunday was her day off too, and we'd go to the local coffee bar for gossip.

The following summer, after I'd turned seventeen, Mrs Hislop sat me down one day for a chat. 'Now, Pet,' she said, 'we'll be going on a family holiday soon for two weeks. Where will you go while we're away?'

I looked at her. 'I beg your pardon?'

'Well,' she continued, 'you can't stay here on your own.'

I don't know what she thought I'd get up to in an empty house – I certainly wouldn't be throwing any wild parties. Anyway, I didn't know anyone except Pauline. I said, 'I've got nowhere to go, Mrs Hislop.'

But she wouldn't budge. 'Well, you'll have to find somewhere,' she said firmly. End of conversation.

I couldn't wait to see Pauline the following Sunday to ask her advice about what I should do. I couldn't go and stay in her house – her employers wouldn't have allowed it. But Pauline had a friend, an older woman of about thirty called Lily Keegan who worked as a silver service waitress in the Hoylake Hotel at West Kirby in the Wirral. Lily, said Pauline, would be able to help me out. She gave her a call and the three of us arranged to meet the following Sunday. As luck would have it, said Lily, there was a vacancy at the hotel on Reception. Lily would put in a word for me. I didn't know what to say. I was grateful for her kindness but I'd had no education to speak of. I'd never used a typewriter. I'd never had to deal with bills and money. 'Oh, don't be daft,' said Lily. 'You'll pick it up soon enough.'

So she went and had a word with the owners, the Johnsons, and, sure enough I was offered the job. It was only a week before the Hislops went off on holiday, so I was cutting it fine. But first I had to go and tell Mrs Hislop I was moving out.

'Moving out, Pet?' she said in amazement. 'What on earth do you mean?'

I explained that I'd had to find another live-in job because I wasn't going to be allowed to stay in her house while the family was away.

'Well,' she said, 'why don't you work in this hotel for the two weeks we're away and then come back to me?'

I shook my head. I wasn't going to do that. It wasn't fair on the Johnsons and, anyway, I hadn't created this situation – she had. 'And I'd be faced with the same problem,' I said, 'the next time you decide to go away.'

She was very huffy about it all. But she'd left me with no choice.

I'd been right, though, about working as a receptionist. I just wasn't up to it. One of my tasks was to type out that day's menu each morning. I didn't know where to begin. Then there were various clerical books I was meant to keep up-to-date – simple enough as I look back now, but beyond my capabilities then. I was getting myself into a terrible state. No one likes to get up each day to a job they know they can't do. I'd sit at the typewriter, tears pouring down my face. I was desperate because I knew I had nowhere else to go. And then Lily would breeze by. 'How're you doing, love?' I'd say that I just couldn't cope and she'd tell me not to worry; it would sort itself out.

I had my own room down a corridor where all the chambermaids lived. There was lots of company, which I liked, but I was living on my nerves because I knew I was failing at my work. At the end of my second week, the Johnsons' son came and had a word with me.

'I'm very sorry, Pat,' he said. 'I'm going to have to let you go. You can't manage the job, love, can you?'

I admitted I was out of my depth and asked if he had work as a chambermaid. I'd always known how to clean.

But there were no vacancies. He said he'd give me an extra week's wages, but that I must leave the following day.

'But I've got nowhere to go,' I protested.

It was no good; he wouldn't be persuaded. 'I'm sorry, love,' he said, 'but there's nothing I can do.'

Now I was in a real panic and I could feel my heart thumping away. A few minutes later, Lily walked through Reception. 'How're you doing?' she asked in her usual breezy way. 'Oh, Lily,' I said, 'I've just been fired. I've got to leave in the morning.'

She stopped in her tracks. 'Christ!' she exclaimed. 'Well, I won't see you out on the street. Leave it to me. When you've packed up your things tomorrow, come along to my room and you can stay there while we think of something else.' She was a good woman.

On the Saturday morning I did as I was told and crept along the corridor, then knocked gently on her door and she let me in. We had to be as quiet as mice because her room was very near the Johnsons' own suite. She sat me down, told me not to make a sound, and said she'd be back later with something to eat from the kitchen. She was taking a big risk. No one was allowed to eat in their rooms – they had to use the staff canteen. If Lily got caught, she'd lose her job. Throughout that day and the next she brought me up bits and bobs to eat as I stared at the four walls. It had to be cold food – not that I minded – because, as Lily explained, hot food would make the room smell and that might have given the game away. I'd only go to the bathroom after dark, for fear of someone spotting me. At night, we slept top-to-tail in her single bed.

This couldn't carry on. After two days and two nights she told me she had a friend in Wales, a man called Bill Davies who worked as a commercial rep supplying chemists' shops. He was a twenty-eight-year-old bachelor with an eye for the ladies. 'I'll have a word with Taff,' she said. That's what she called him. 'He knows everybody and all the hotels. He'll get you fixed up.' And she was true to her word. Late on the evening of my third day hiding in Lily's room, she led me on tiptoe down the back stairs of the Hoylake Hotel and into Bill Davies's waiting car. I was a tall, blonde, seventeen-year-old virgin. I think he must have thought all his Christmases had come at once.

It's funny the perceptions some people have of themselves. Bill obviously considered himself God's gift to women, but in reality he was a very plain man with precious little personality. As so often in my life, though, what choice did I have? He drove me to Betws-y-coed, his home town in north Wales, and took me to the Royal Oak, a hotel run by old friends of his. He had a word with the manageress, who said she had a vacancy as a junior receptionist. My heart sank. I told Bill I just wasn't qualified for that type of work. 'Look, she's a nice woman,' he said. 'See how you get along.' And it did mean I had somewhere to lay my head.

I knew from the start that Bill wasn't going to all this trouble just out of the kindness of his heart: he made that pretty obvious. If we were sitting in a pub or driving in his car his hands would be all over me. I wasn't attracted to him in the least, but I began to run out of ways to refuse him. My instincts for survival, which were well-honed by then, also told me that I had to find myself a job I could do properly before I turned my back on him. If I carried on saying no he'd dump me – and then where would I be? But I'd never so much as kissed a boy, far less slept with anyone. And the prospect of sex with Bill Davies in particular did the very opposite to filling me with lust. All I felt was anxiety.

One day he drove the car up a track away from the main road and we climbed into the back. I still think of what happened next with a shiver of revulsion. I'd told him I was a virgin, but he wasn't remotely interested in how I was feeling or any discomfort I might be experiencing; he was only thinking of his own satisfaction. To add insult to injury, he asked me afterwards why I hadn't told him the truth. He said he could tell I wasn't a virgin. But of course I knew I was. It was only later I discovered that not all women bleed when they first have sex. Looking back, it's a wonder I didn't get pregnant. I was completely ignorant of contraception and Bill I now realise, never bothered with it. Anyway, from that day on every time he took me out we ended up in the back of his car having sex. In the circumstances, what option did I have?

Ten days into the job, it was obvious that my lack of experience still didn't qualify me for Reception work. But then I'd never been trained in typing or book-keeping or looking after petty cash. When Bill came to collect me to take me out that evening I poured out my feelings about not being able to cope with the job, and told him that I knew the manageress of the Royal Oak was about to sack me. Bill seemed to know everyone in north Wales, and he said he'd introduce me to some friends at Cobden's Hotel in a place called Capel Curig, about ten minutes from Betws-y-coed. The owner turned out to be an oldish man who ran what seemed more like a haunted house than a hotel. But he did have a vacancy for a waitress, so at least I wouldn't have to worry whether I was up to the job.

After a while, I was given to understand that the much younger man who helped run the place was the boyfriend of the owner. They were like an old married couple, bickering all the time and constantly having lovers' tiffs. I'd hear the older man calling from their bedroom, 'Oh, come back to bed, come back. I love you.' He was drunk half the time and always grumpy, but then he was probably hungover each morning.

This all came as a bit of a revelation to me. I'd never met a gay couple before; to be truthful, I didn't even know homosexuality existed. Two men sleeping in the same bed and doing their version of what a man and a woman did? I thought the waiter, Ion, who told me about the owner and his boyfriend was pulling my leg. In the environment in which I'd been raised homosexuals didn't exist or, if they did, they must have kept their sexuality extremely well-hidden because I'd never even heard it discussed. In my room at night, I'd turn it all over in my mind. It wasn't that I was disgusted – more that I was mystified. I just didn't understand it.

The hotel could have been lovely, but the owner had let it deteriorate and there were never many guests. There was even a rumour that it was going to be put up for sale. But the work was easy and in my time off I liked going over the bridge to the Capel Curig rocks and sitting with the water rushing over my feet. In the end, though, the rows between the owner and his boyfriend became so bad that I made up my mind to move on. Up till now I'd spent my whole life surrounded by people fighting and screaming. Enough was enough.

One of the other girls who worked there happened one day to mention a holiday camp at Prestatyn in Denbighshire, run by Bluecoats, which would be taking on staff for the summer season. This girl had worked there the previous season. It was good money, she said, and there were lots of young people working there, a real cross-section of society. All meals were free for the two hundred or so staff, who also had their own bar – and there was a good social scene. So I asked Bill if he'd give me a lift – it was about an hour's drive away – to see if I could get taken on for the summer. It wasn't long after my eighteenth birthday.

They had lots of jobs going, and I had no trouble being taken on as a waitress. I handed in my notice at Cobden's and moved to Prestatyn in April 1960. It felt like joining the circus. There were lots of people my own age, and groups of us would go to one of the local pubs when we were off duty. At mealtimes we waitresses would serve the same people at the same four or five tables throughout their stay, and then get a big tip from each family at the end of their week or fortnight.

I had to share a chalet with three other girls, which I didn't particularly like – I've always jealously guarded my privacy. There were two pairs of bunk beds, and we each had our own wardrobe. But I was happier than I'd been in a long time – especially as Bill Davies never turned up at my door again. I think he'd found other fish to fry, and you wouldn't have heard me complaining. There were lots of young men working at the camp, but I wasn't interested in getting a boyfriend. Sex with Bill hadn't exactly attracted me to the idea of looking for more of the same. There was one boy, a lovely lad and very lanky, called Andy. I knew he liked me because he'd confided in one of the other girls who'd then told me. But I was just happy to do my job, earn a bit of money and have a laugh. It was almost as if I was living the childhood I'd never had.

In fact I enjoyed myself so much that I didn't want the season to come to an end. When September came round, I knew I had to try to join the skeleton staff that looked after the camp in the winter. But then I had an accident. A couple of weeks before the end of the season there was a staff party in the canteen. Everyone was getting a bit merry. There was a particular boy called Brian who I knew was sweet on me, and we were both larking about. When I ran back towards my chalet he gave chase and, just as I got through the door, pushed it hard against me; my right hand went straight through the glass. There was blood everywhere.

The tip of the middle finger of my right hand was sliced clean off, and to this day I've got a large scar on my right forearm.

Brian panicked at first, but he did then take me to the resident doctor who stitched me up. I didn't want to get him into trouble, because we'd both been mucking about and he'd never intended to hurt me. But my injuries meant I was off work for two weeks; I couldn't do my job as a waitress with my right arm and hand out of action. I was paid until the end of the season, but what then? I looked in the papers, but there were no jobs in north Wales during the winter. What was I going to do?

There was nothing for it. I'd have to get in touch with my father and ask if I could come and stay with him and Betty. And that was the very last thing on this earth that I wanted to do.

10

A Home of My Own

I didn't recognise the man's voice at the other end of the phone. 'Is that the Horse and Jockey?' I asked. The man told me it was. So I asked to speak to my father.

'Your dad doesn't live here any more,' he said. 'And he doesn't work here, either. He lives across the road in a rented cottage.' Then he gave me his number. I couldn't imagine what must have happened. It was a beautiful pub with more rooms than you could fill. Had there been some falling out with the brewery? Had my father had his hand in the till?

My parents were always saying things behind each other's backs, and I remember my mother saying that my father was light-fingered. He'd once been the quartermaster when he was stationed at Eastney Barracks, and I saw with my own eyes the enormous box he brought home, stuffed to overflowing with chocolates and sweets and jars of fancy food. The war might have been over but there was still rationing, and I knew Dad hadn't bought this stuff with his own money. There was later an enquiry when it was realised what had gone missing, but according to my mother my father wasn't even questioned. Everyone was simply given new duties, and that was the end of it. So perhaps my father had been on the fiddle in the Horse and Jockey; or maybe he'd been watering the whisky and then selling what he'd siphoned off. To this day I don't know, because he wouldn't ever tell me honestly why he had to leave. Whatever the reason, something had gone wrong. He wasn't the sort to give up a good job without lining another one up.

'Oh yes,' he said when I rang his new number. 'We left the pub. We got sick of the hours.'

I knew he was lying but what could I say? Later on he became the tenant of another pub – he obviously hadn't been put off by the hours there. I told him I needed to come and live with him in the cottage until I found another job, explaining that it wouldn't be for long and that I'd pay him for my accommodation out of my holiday camp earnings. He didn't have much choice. Although I'd never have told Betty about what had happened, my dad didn't know that. I couldn't help marvelling at the irony. My father had attempted to molest me, and because of that he had no option but to offer me a roof over my head. It was just as well – otherwise I'd have been out on the street. I caught the train back to Upton.

The cottage was tiny and we were all living cheek by jowl, but not once did my father ever do or say anything inappropriate to me. And I think Betty was grateful for the rent I paid her out of my savings. It was while I was staying there that I celebrated my nineteenth birthday. Betty bought me a little bottle of perfume. And for only the second time in my life – the other occasion had been my sixteenth birthday, just after I'd run away from home and thrown myself on my father's mercy – he gave me a birthday card. It's a long time ago now, and I only read the verse in that card a couple of times, but I still remember every word. On the front there was a drawing of a little girl wearing an old-fashioned crinoline dress and a bonnet. Inside, the verse read:

> I sometimes wonder if you know
> How much one little thought of you
> Can help to make the passing hours
> Far brighter and more happy, too?
>
> I wonder if you know how much
> You're in my thoughts from day to day
> And just how much I'm wishing you
> The best of luck along life's way?

I remember reading it and thinking, *You two-faced so-and-so! How dare you send me a card that's so pretty, so thoughtful and so phoney!* I vowed that from that day forward I would never send a card – be it Christmas or birthday – if I didn't feel sincere about the verse inside. I'd sooner send an ugly card if I believed in the words.

I couldn't live off my savings indefinitely and so, while I looked for something more permanent that would pay me enough to be able to afford a place of my own, I worked for a short while at Woolworth's in nearby Morton, near to Cadbury's chocolate factory. Once again I was put on the toiletries counter, not my favourite part of the store, but the other girls were good fun. None of them became close friends, but we'd go into Liverpool on our days off and look at the shops or go to the fair. A little later I saw an ad in the paper for people to work on the conveyor belt at the Meccano toy factory on Binns Road in Liverpool. I liked the look of the set-up there and took a job.

Then I had to find myself somewhere to live. I couldn't afford anywhere nice, but even now I shudder when I think of what I had to settle for. Kingsley Road is in Liverpool 8, an area notorious then for its pimps and prostitutes. For one pound ten shillings a week, I had what I can only describe as the cellar of a large Victorian terraced house that had seen much better days. It was really no more than a dosshouse. As soon as I opened the front door, my nostrils were filled with the dank, musty smell. The carpet in the hall was filthy. People often ask me how I can bear to put my hands down some of the filthy toilets I have to scrub on *How Clean Is Your House?* And the answer is simple. If you've lived in some of the places I've had to live in, no amount of dirt bothers you any more. Anyway, my desire to have everything spotless is paramount.

The basement had never been converted into proper living accommodation; it was where the meters were kept. There was a dirty old bed under a mantelpiece with a gas meter on it. The door of the battered wardrobe was hanging off. Scraps of newspaper were stuck to the surface of the table where people had spilt their food and drink over the years. The so-called kitchen was no more than a cooker shoved up against a wall. A disgusting sink stood in one corner, and a big wooden box-type affair served as the toilet. It was, quite simply, a hovel, but I cleaned and cleaned and cleaned that place until my hands were red raw. It was never going to look good, but when I'd finished I knew there wasn't a speck of dirt or dust to be found anywhere. I've never lived in worse accommodation before or since. But it was cheap, I had to live somewhere and it was at least mine.

I didn't know the other tenants, although I did see the people who lived on the ground floor. In the room at the front there was a woman who must have had some bad accident. She'd only go out after dark, and she wore her black hair in a long fringe in an attempt to cover the scarring all over her face. Even so, she shared the front room with a man. At the back on the ground floor there was a married couple. As I came up my basement stairs into the hall they always opened their door to pass the time of day. I could see past them to a big window in the back wall. I envied them that – I had virtually no natural light in my bedsit.

I hated coming back from the Meccano factory after dark because there were all sorts of shady characters lurking in my road. In fact I was frightened most of the time. I'd go down into the basement and sit huddled on my bed, hardly daring to move about the place because I didn't want to draw attention to myself. Yes, there was a door at the top of the stairs – but it had no lock on it. Anyone could have opened it and walked down into my bedsit. I'd been living there a few months, though, when the married couple moved out and I asked the landlord if I could move in. It was two pounds a week, but it was worth the extra to be out of that dark, depressing basement. As it turned out, it wasn't much better. The small cooker was on a chair at the end of the bed, and the sink was filthy.

Occasionally, I'd go to the pub run by the parents of Sally, one of the girls who worked alongside me at Meccano. It was near the factory and the Littlewood's pools building. We always had a laugh there, and her mum and dad were kind to me. But then so were the supervisors at Meccano who organised glasses to deal with my previously undiscovered poor eyesight. The packaging department, to which I was then transferred, was the 'soft' bit of the operation where the old dears worked – the women who'd been there for years and were nearing retirement. I think they felt sorry for a girl living alone miles from her family, and took me under their wing. They'd bring in pieces of cake and biscuits for me. They were lovely, funny, kind-hearted women, and every day we'd have a good laugh.

I must have lived in the dosshouse – basement and ground floor – for about eighteen months, and all the time I was saving like mad. I'd keep the money in the toe of one of my boots with newspaper stuffed down on top of it. I realise now that I was taking a risk, but it never crossed my mind to open a bank account. I carried on working at Meccano for a few more months, but while I continued to be shown nothing but kindness I knew I couldn't stay for ever. I was determined to make something of my life. I was tall and, rather late in the day, my figure had blossomed: my bust had started to grow and grow. Now, I always say that, if I fell over, I'd strike oil! So I was a five-foot-ten blonde with a curvy figure and, if I say so myself, a nice pair of legs. My appearance was beginning to give me a new sort of confidence. Perhaps I could get some professional training and see if I could make it as a model.

I couldn't afford not to work in the meantime, though, so I got a job as an usherette in a cinema and then enrolled on a six-month course at the Patricia Platt Modelling School in Bold Street. It cost me £50 which I could ill afford and which was a lot of money in those days, but I felt I was investing in my future. Some of the classes were in the day, some in the evening, and it wasn't hard to work them round my shifts at the cinema. Most mothers pass on tips about cosmetics and clothes to their daughters but mine had never bothered. So I had a lot to learn, and I was a willing pupil. We were shown how to walk, how to sit down and stand up again in a ladylike way, how to get out of a car without showing our undies, how to apply make-up correctly – in effect, how to look our best at all times. I loved it. I felt my life was moving in the right direction.

I was also more than ready to move out of

Kingsley Road, so I found a top-floor flat in Ullet Road in Liverpool 15 – not far away but a much nicer area. I had a big lounge with a sink and kitchen in the corner, and a bedroom off it. It cost me two pounds ten shillings a week, quite a lot of money then, but it was worth it. The whole house was kept clean by the landlady. Unfortunately she also lived on the premises, so she was always wanting to know everyone's business. No men were allowed in the house – which didn't really bother me at that stage of my life – but I resented being checked up on all the time. I was nineteen now, and wanted to feel I could come and go as I pleased.

After my course at Patricia Platt finished I got a few local jobs doing catwalk modelling in the larger stores in Liverpool and some catalogue work for Littlewood's. I never made the big time and never would have done; I realise now that you need to be in London if that's ever going to happen. But I made a bit of money along the way and I enjoyed the work when it came along. Anyway, I didn't waste my money on that modelling course because it taught me good deportment and grooming – assets that have remained with me to this day.

Perhaps the best store in Liverpool was Lewis's – six floors of sheer heaven! The lift doors were made of wrought iron and painted with gold leaf. There were fabulous restaurants. There were marble pillars. To me, it was a palace. So when I saw an advertisement for a cosmetician to work in the beauty hall I didn't hesitate. And, because of my experience at Patricia Platt, I got the job. I really thought I'd arrived. I was put on the perfumery counter and told, as were all the other girls, that I must always look perfectly groomed. On a Saturday afternoon there was a constant stream of men who found themselves lost in Lewis's beauty hall, accidentally on purpose, as they eyed up the glamorous assistants.

In time I moved to the counter that sold Dorothy Gray skin creams, which were really classy, and I stayed there some months. Then one of the other girls said that you could earn much more money as a freelance in-store demonstrator selling particular products and making most of your money on commission. Apparently they were looking for someone to sell what are known as carousel combs – round, open-toothed combs that clip into a circle and pull your hair off your face. I thought I'd give it a try. I've always had a flair for selling, and of course it brought out the performer in me. I half-imagined I was standing on a stage with passing customers as my audience. 'Come along, girls,' I'd cry. 'Come and get your carousel combs!' It was rather demeaning after what I'd been used to, but it was very good money. Ronson then employed me to sell their lighters, both in Lewis's and Owen Owen's, another department store across the road. I sold more Ronson lighters than you could shake a stick at and I was earning three times what the assistants were getting.

So as a result of that I moved out of Ullet Road and into my own full-sized apartment at the top of a house not far away in Brompton Avenue. Things were really starting to look up. I was twenty. I went out on dates, mostly with men who came into the store and started chatting me up. I didn't mind – I felt I could look after myself. I was taken out for drinks and I was bought nice meals. I should have been happy and carefree. And yet I was still possessed by a feeling of loneliness that I couldn't shake off. You can be in a room full of people and still feel alone. And I certainly hadn't yet met anyone whom I thought I'd want to share my life with.

By the time I was twenty-two I occasionally went out with a boy called Stuart – nothing serious. Then one day he brought a friend of his called John to my flat. I liked John immediately. He was good-looking, with blonde hair, and he seemed fun even though he'd had quite a sad life. His father had died before John was born and his mother had also died young. So he'd been brought up by his mother's sister and her husband in a well-to-do area north of Liverpool where he still lived. He worked as a rep and he was always in and out of the stores where I worked.

We fell in love; at least, I thought it was love. He was certainly the first boy I'd ever had any real feelings for. It was hardly surprising that I responded to someone who, for the first time in my life, showed me some real affection. I was looking for something I'd never had. Could this be it? To begin with, I really thought John might be the one. We started going around with other couples and soon I seemed to be part of a circle, something completely unfamiliar to me. We might all hire speed boats for the day, or go into the country to a pub or for a picnic. I ate out all the time, either in a crowd or just with John. Gradually I acquired the sort of life that other people took for granted.

My relationship with John quickly became physical and he often stayed overnight with me; we never slept together at his aunt and uncle's. I can't say now if what we had was love, but I do know he satisfied a need in me as the weeks stretched into months. Before long, or so it seemed, we'd been going out together for two years – and that's when things slowly began to change. John had always been very kind and I trusted him absolutely. But somehow he didn't seem quite as keen any more. He made excuses for not staying over. He bought me fewer bunches of flowers. I knew something was wrong.

I told myself that the novelty had worn off but if I ever asked him whether there was some sort of problem he'd immediately tell me I was being silly. Men aren't always very good at telling the truth about their feelings. But then, women can delude themselves. When you imagine yourself to be in love, you can be blind to the obvious. I wanted to believe the best of him. By now I'd been taken on by Carmen to demonstrate and sell their heated rollers which meant travelling all over the country. John had a key to my flat, and I'd told him it was fine for him to stay there if he wanted to when I was out of Liverpool. On one occasion I got back after a spell in Bournemouth and found all the framed photographs of myself with John turned face-down on my dressing-table. Naïve as I was, it took me a little while to work out why John wouldn't want pictures of the two of us on display.

My suspicions were later to prove well-founded, but at the time I didn't know what to think. I might have been full of confidence when it came to persuading people to buy perfume or cosmetics or heated rollers in department stores, but I still lacked it in my personal relationships. My dream was simple: I wanted a happy life. That made me gullible and prepared to believe John when I asked him about the photo frames. He'd just been dusting them, he said. I know that sounds ridiculous – what young man is going to dust his girlfriend's flat in her absence? – but he was very convincing. Was I really accusing him of cheating on me? What sort of a person did I think he was? Was I seriously suggesting he'd ever contemplate sleeping with another girl and in my bed, the bed he and I had shared so often? He went on so long and so effectively that I ended up thinking I was the daft one – and feeling guilty, too, for harbouring these suspicions.

But I couldn't deceive myself about what I felt in my heart – we were drifting apart. I came to accept that this relationship might not go the full distance. The more I thought about it, the sadder I became. And I was terribly hurt that John couldn't sit down with me and either talk through whatever he saw as our problems or have the guts to tell me he wanted to move on.

So what happened next was bad timing, to say the least. I was twenty-three, with a relationship that seemed to be heading for the rocks and, as I was about to discover, three months pregnant.

11

The Worst Night of My Life

In the late summer of 1965 John and I had booked a holiday to Barcelona – the first time I'd ever been out of England, the first time I'd ever been on a plane. We were going with two other couples: Michael and Sally, and Alan and Christine. At that time, even for Spain you had to have an injection six weeks before you went. The doctor told me that a few days later a small lump would appear in my armpit, but I should ignore it and it would soon go away.

I really enjoyed seeing another country but I can't say the holiday was a total success. John was good fun when we were all together in a group, but as soon as we were alone I could sense a coolness. We'd been going out for almost three years. Until fairly recently he'd been staying at my place on Brompton Avenue for four or five nights a week, but then it had started to dwindle to one or two. There was a reason for that: I found out later he'd begun seeing a girl called Anne. When he wasn't with me, he was with her. I was the last one to know what was going on, although I wouldn't be surprised if Anne knew nothing about me either.

I suppose I just thought he was being a bit moody, and because I knew he was fed up with his job I decided to do something for him. In one of the stores I'd got friendly with a girl whose father was about to launch his own line in skin creams, and he offered me a job running the office he was setting up in Liverpool. To be honest, I didn't fancy working behind a desk. But I did think it would be the perfect solution to John's problems. It was good money, he had the right experience and if we were going to get married one day – as I still secretly hoped we might – I thought he should have the security of this much better job. And to cap it all there'd be no travel, which I knew was beginning to get him down in his job as a rep. So I recommended John and they took him on. He was grateful, but still the old warmth between us seemed to be missing.

Then, shortly after getting home from Spain, I missed a period. That was extremely unusual for me; in fact, I couldn't remember it ever happening before. But the mind plays tricks. I didn't feel different in any way so maybe I wasn't pregnant after all. And the prospect of John finishing our relationship filled me with dread – perhaps the anxiety had caused me to miss my period. I tried to put the thought out of my mind and get on with my life. I wouldn't have to wait too long to see if my worst suspicions were going to be confirmed.

A month later I missed another period and, although I still had no feelings of nausea or any other physical signs, I had to face facts: I must be pregnant. So I waited till John and I were alone together in my flat and told him my news. His reaction was strange. He didn't ask me to marry him – to be honest, I hadn't really expected that. But he didn't seem either particularly pleased or particularly upset. He was almost expressionless, non-committal. I suppose he already knew – not that he'd yet told me – that we wouldn't be together much longer and that I'd have to make any decisions about the future of the pregnancy on my own. If he'd been truthful about his intentions it would have been a shock, the very last thing I wanted in the circumstances, but it would also have given me a chance to adjust to being on my own. But, like all too many men, he took the easy route and put off saying what he knew in his heart. Looking back now, I can see he was rather a cold fish.

He never mentioned anything about an abortion, though. But then he knew me well.

Individual people must make their individual decisions and I would never sit in judgement. But, equally, there is no way I could have got rid of my baby. It wasn't the baby's fault that the mother was having a rotten time, and I couldn't have taken the life of that little soul. I'd no idea how I'd manage with a baby to bring up, with or without John. It would probably be a struggle, but then I'd struggled all my life. This would be just one more – but one, I thought, that would be so very worthwhile. I hadn't meant to get pregnant and I think it took me those first three months to get over the shock of it. Now I was beginning to feel a sense of excitement shot through with panic at what lay ahead, and whether I'd be able to cope. At three months, I went to my local GP. I was very embarrassed about my situation but I had to know for sure. He confirmed the pregnancy.

John was still being rather cool with me, but we were at least together. An even bigger shock was in store, though. Three weeks later we met our holiday companions Michael and Sally and Alan and Christine for a drink in a pub. Suddenly John said, 'That bloody lump in my armpit still hasn't gone down, you know.'

We all looked at him. Michael said his own lump had disappeared weeks ago; and the same had been true for the rest of us. With that, John rolled up his shirtsleeve and showed us a lump the size of a duck's egg. 'Bloody hell!' said Michael. 'You ought to go and see a doctor, mate.'

The next day John was rushed into hospital where the lump was removed, and he had to stay there for about three weeks before being allowed home. He didn't tell me what was wrong with him at the time, but I knew he was very ill – otherwise why were they giving him radiation treatment? I'd go and visit him in hospital in Bootle. He'd joke about it, but you could see that underneath he was terrified. One day, I plucked up courage. Please would he tell me exactly what was wrong with him?

It was cancer, he said, a form that often affects people in their early twenties. Whether the injection had somehow triggered it was never made clear. He seemed so young to be struck down by something so serious. But I think his youth worked in his favour in the end, because he appeared to make a good recovery.

I was worried sick. I was pregnant, my boyfriend had cancer, and even if he got well again I couldn't be certain whether he was going to stick by me. John's attitude seemed to be that I might well have problems but at least I knew I was going to be alive to deal with them. That may have been true – but it didn't stop everything from getting on top of me, and my hair had started falling out again. I needed to confide in someone. Michael and Sally were good friends to me and I decided to tell them my secret – it helped to share the burden. When I talked to them they made me feel that, whatever happened between me and John, they'd help in any way they could when the baby finally arrived.

As it happens, the pregnancy itself wasn't proving difficult. I was blooming although my figure hadn't changed at all. No one meeting me could possibly have guessed that I was pregnant, and I was still able to wear the same fitted skirts to work each day. I was now selling perfumery and cosmetics at Affleck and Brown, a department store in Deansgate, Manchester; I commuted there daily by train from Liverpool Lime Street.

When I was four months pregnant John sat me down one day in my flat for the conversation I'd prayed wouldn't ever happen, the one I'd been dreading. He'd met someone else, he said, and he didn't want to see me any more. My instinctive reaction was to break down in tears. I cried and cried as John sat there. But quite quickly I also felt anger rising in me. I was furious at the way things were happening. Life is complicated but I felt that I deserved more respect. 'You can't leave me now,' I wailed, like an actress in a bad movie. It was an awful moment for me.

He wasn't a cruel man in any way but whatever he felt for this other girl was more powerful than any feelings he might have had for me. I could see I was fighting a losing battle, and I just wanted him out of my flat. Later, alone with my thoughts, I began to feel really scared about the future. Now I knew for sure that I'd be bringing up my baby on my own. I told myself over and over that I could handle this situation alone, but as I lay in my bed in Brompton Avenue waves of panic washed over me. Would I really be able to manage when the time came?

The next day I told Michael and Sally what John had said, and they admitted they'd known about Anne. It had placed them in a very difficult situation, they said. After I'd told John about my pregnancy, I think they'd hoped he would finish with Anne and stand by me. When I was a little girl and wondered if I would ever have a child of my own one day, I always imagined him or her having a loving mother and father – something I'd never known. So I was anxious at the prospect of the poor little soul being brought up by a single parent in a small flat. But what was the alternative? And we'd survive. I'd make sure of that.

I still couldn't get over the way that John had treated me. Then, to add insult to injury, two friends of ours got married. I was invited and so was John. I didn't think he'd turn up, knowing I was going to be there. But he did – and with Anne on his arm! I was so hurt. I couldn't even look at him. I certainly didn't speak to him. I so wanted to know if he'd told Anne that I was pregnant by him, but I couldn't bring myself to ask him.

Fortunately I did have good, loyal friends. Sally, a pretty little thing who looked like a young Petula Clark, and was the nearest I had to a best friend; Michael looked the spit of John Lennon. Sally was always there for me. She often invited me to her parents' house on a Sunday for roast dinner cooked by her mother. She and Michael lived with her parents, although they weren't married at that stage. But her parents could see that Michael was the right man for their only child, and eventually, they did marry. There was also a nice boy in our circle of friends called Harry. I'd told him about my situation and he was very kind to me. He told me that if I needed cheering up I'd only got to call him, and he'd take me out for a meal and a chat. It was friendship, no more than that, but good all the same.

I was now about five and a half months pregnant – and still it didn't show. One evening I went out to a restaurant with Michael and Sally, after which they dropped me back at Brompton Avenue. As I was climbing the stairs I suddenly became aware of warm water running down my legs. I couldn't understand what was going on. It had happened without warning; I hadn't felt ill. I couldn't be going into labour – not at five and a half months. And the pregnancy had been going so smoothly. In my flat, I took off my damp clothes and tried to stay calm. There hadn't been much water – maybe that was why I wasn't looking pregnant – so perhaps it was a false alarm. Or maybe I'd simply wet myself. The trouble was, I was pretty ignorant about my condition. Except for going to my GP to have the pregnancy confirmed, I'd had no antenatal care of any kind. I realise now how foolish that was, but from the start I'd been so embarrassed by my condition. In those days there was still a definite social stigma attached to a woman who got pregnant outside marriage.

I sat down on my bed feeling absolutely fine, but something had happened and I couldn't ignore it. I wasn't suffering any pain, though, and I was too ashamed to take myself to the hospital to find out if anything was wrong. I didn't know what to do for the best. And then the doorbell rang. It was Harry, who'd seen my light on. I buzzed him in, and he asked how I was getting on.

I said, 'You can't stay. I think something's happened.'

When I explained the situation to him, he found it hard to believe. 'Are you sure?' he said. It was too early in my pregnancy, and anyway I looked so good. Surely I'd be suffering if the baby was on the way?

I may have looked fine physically, but what Harry didn't know was that I'd been anxious ever since my pregnancy had been confirmed. My thoughts would swing from imagining holding my newborn baby in my arms to worrying desperately about our uncertain future together. Instead of putting on weight I'd been losing it. I'd also started to vomit a sort of yellow bile. Of course I should have gone to the doctor weeks earlier but, nice though he was, I knew I wouldn't be able to face him. Apart from the embarrassment I was crying all the time, and I was worried I'd break down in front of him.

But maybe Harry's *right*, I thought. I'd lost a little water, but perhaps that could sometimes happen during a pregnancy. We were both ignorant about what was going on. The difference, though, was that it was happening to me. Harry couldn't have been kinder, but after a while I told him I'd rather be on my own and with great reluctance he left, making me promise to get in touch if the situation changed.

As soon as he'd gone I started getting ready for

bed. It was only about ten o'clock, but I liked to be in bed early because I always had to be up first thing in the morning for the journey to Manchester. I sat on the edge of my bed and bent down to take off my slippers. Suddenly, a sharp pain shot through my abdomen. I knew I couldn't cry out because there were other tenants in the house, and I didn't want them to come knocking on my door. I struggled up from the bed and stumbled towards the lounge. The pain was excruciating. But still I wouldn't scream. I grabbed a handful of paper tissues and stuffed them into my mouth to muffle sound.

Less than half an hour earlier I'd more or less convinced myself that everything was fine. Not any longer. *Please God*, I prayed, *don't say the baby's coming*. Sweat was pouring off me by now and my body was drenched as the pain kept sweeping over me. I managed to get all my clothes off before the next stabbing surge of pain made me grab the side of the sink for support. I was in agony, but throughout it all I managed to bite back my screams.

Another pain ripped through my body and made me bend almost double. I looked down, and that's when I saw a baby's foot sticking out from between my legs. I thought I was going to faint, but then my mind briefly cleared. I'd read somewhere that babies don't turn in the womb until they're at least six months old. My little baby was coming out feet first. I'd never been more frightened or in so much pain in my life. What was I going to do? I took the washing-up bowl from the sink, threw it on the floor and stood straddled across it.

Then I got hold of a tea towel, wrapped it around the little foot and gently eased it further out of my body. Almost at once, the other foot dropped out. I was beside myself. The feet looked tiny, but not as small as I'd have thought. Maybe I'd been further into the pregnancy than I'd realised. Maybe my baby might be born alive. I had to get it out as quickly as possible for it to have a chance. I didn't want to touch the baby's skin with my bare hands for fear of harming it; anyway, my hands were soaked in sweat and I was frightened I might drop it. So I wrapped the towel round both feet and pulled and pulled, firmly but gently, until the rest of the baby gradually appeared. It was a boy, and I could tell he was dead straightaway. There wasn't a flicker of life in him. His eyes weren't much more than slits, and yet the rest of him was perfectly formed. I just stared and stared at the tiny bundle in my hands.

That poor little soul: he was so beautiful. There was no sign of breathing, but he had such perfect little legs and hands. Then I noticed the cord. In my ignorance I didn't think he'd have a cord because he was so little. That was nonsense, of course, because how else could he have been fed? But I was young and inexperienced, and living through the most horrendous nightmare of my life did nothing for my mental faculties. Nevertheless I knew the cord had to be cut so I reached for a pair of scissors from the drawer, closed my eyes and snipped straight through it. Still holding my baby in the tea towel, I lowered him gently into the bowl. The pain persisted and then, after what must have been another contraction, the afterbirth appeared – not that I knew what it was at the time. I put it in the bowl with the baby.

I was bleeding heavily – but it wasn't only that. In hospital, I'd have been given an enema before I gave birth. Without one, throughout this nightmare experience I hadn't been able to control my other bodily functions. I was soiled from the waist down, in a terrible state.

Time passed, and slowly my body started to calm down. All I could do was sit and stare at my dear little boy. I kept thinking, over and over, that this couldn't have happened to me. I hadn't known how my baby and I would have managed if he'd been born when he was meant to be. But somehow I knew we'd have been all right. We'd have coped, him and me against the world. And now this.

For the moment, though, I knew I had to start

cleaning myself up. I stood at the sink and began to wash my whole body from top to toe. I was still bleeding, but now it was little worse than a heavy period; a sanitary towel soon absorbed the blood. Even so, I was worried I might need stitches – but still I decided to see how it went. I wouldn't call an ambulance. I couldn't face letting anyone know what had happened.

I don't know why, but I then picked up the bowl containing the baby and put it beside my bed. I lay down, my mind all over the place, as I tried to work out what to do. I felt so weak and exhausted – both physically and emotionally drained. But I knew I had to deal with this on my own. I had my dead baby beside me. He wasn't going to go away. What was I going to do with him?

I must have dozed off without realising it, because when I opened my eyes again it was quarter to seven in the morning. My first thought was that I must go to work. I know how crazy that now sounds, but in my deluded state I think I was trying to carry on as if nothing had happened. Indeed, had all of this really happened? Maybe when I got home again I'd realise I'd been mistaken – or find, in some magical way, that my little boy had somehow sprung into life. In my heart I knew that was a vain hope, but I'd been through a hideous trauma and I just wasn't thinking straight.

So I got up and had a cool bath. I was still bleeding, although not so badly. I expected to feel sore but I didn't. I can scarcely believe this now, but I got dressed and went to Liverpool Lime Street where I caught the nine o'clock train to Manchester. At Affleck and Brown I kept going to the toilet to check that everything was all right, that no blood was leaking on to my clothes. I was pretending everything was fine, which had been my way of dealing with life for as long as I could remember. If you suppress the bad things, then maybe they'll go away – that's what I always used to tell myself. But everything was far from fine: I was exhausted. By two o'clock in the afternoon I could no longer keep up the pretence in front of the other staff that everything was all right. So I told the supervisor I wasn't feeling at all well and asked if I could go home. She was fine about it, and I knew I could have three days off without having to get a doctor's certificate.

But on the journey back to Liverpool, I realised I couldn't face going into the little flat containing my deadly secret. So I went straight from the station to my great friends Michael and Sally's. Throughout my life I'd kept all my dark secrets to myself, surrounding myself with an invisible shield, never telling anyone about the beatings and abuse at home, never sharing my innermost feelings with anyone. It had got to the stage where I felt that I could deal with anything life threw at me on my own. But this was different. This was simply too big, too traumatic an event not to share with my best friends.

Luckily, both Michael and Sally were at home. As soon as I was alone with them, I blurted out my terrible story. 'You'll find this hard to believe,' I said. 'And I can barely believe it myself. But last night I had the baby.'

They were horrified – and full of questions. When did it happen? Was I all right? Had I seen a doctor? Where was the baby now? I told them he was in a washing-up bowl beside my bed. Sally offered to come with me to the flat, but I refused at first. This, I said, was something I had to handle on my own. But she and Michael were obviously terribly worried about me, and in the end I let them drive me home and come inside with me.

When the three of us walked into my bedroom and I showed them my poor dead little boy they were totally shocked. Michael took me in his arms. 'God help you,' he said, his face as white as a sheet. 'God help you.'

But I didn't feel I could involve them any further. They implored me to let them stay; they kept saying that it was too much for me to cope with on my own. But this was my child, my problem, and I had to do it alone. So I asked them to leave, but promised to talk to them in the morning.

Michael later told me that he'd gone straight round to John's after he'd seen the body of the baby and told him what had happened. John was obviously shocked. He offered to go and see me.

'I think it's a bit late for that,' said Michael. 'I'd stay well away if I was you.' And he did, which looking back, I'm sure was for the best.

Alone in the flat, I tried to work out what to do next. I knew exactly what I should have done. My doctor was a kind man and I felt sure he wouldn't have judged me for what had happened. I should have picked up the phone and asked him to come and see me and my dead baby. But I still wasn't thinking straight, and in my confused state felt it was something for me alone.

I waited until it was dark – late in the evening when most people would be indoors. Then I wrapped the baby and the placenta in the tea towel and took a large spoon out of the kitchen drawer. There were a number of parks within walking distance of where I lived, and I chose the one I liked best. It was well-lit at the entrance, but it was large and so it was easy to find a secluded, shady spot where I knew I wouldn't be seen.

I put the baby on the ground and then got down on my knees and started digging into the earth as deeply as I could with the spoon. Tears were streaming down my face and I brushed them away with my dirty hands. When I felt I'd dug deep enough, I lowered my precious little boy and the placenta into the hole and wrapped the towel around him before slowly replacing the earth. But even though the job was done, I couldn't leave. I had so much to say to my darling son.

I told him I was so sorry for what had happened and how great we'd have been together. I told him he'd have been a fine boy but that it just wasn't to be. I'd never felt more wretched in my whole life. I felt I'd been cruel somehow to this innocent child, that I'd treated him badly. And I was consumed by anger with John.

It was a cold February night, although I wasn't aware of the temperature. But I knew I couldn't stay there indefinitely; someone might see me when dawn started to break. I had no alternative but to return home, although I honestly don't know how my feet got me there. But I never returned to that park; I just couldn't bring myself to go there.

Back in the flat, my mind started racing nineteen to the dozen. Would I be punished for the rest of my life for what had happened? How was I ever going to forget this terrible experience? Could I ever get the picture of my baby out of my mind? Would I ever be able to pick up the pieces? I was in the very pit of despair. I never felt the fact that my son hadn't survived was somehow for the best. It was a terrible loss to me, and it seemed to make no sense. Things happen for a reason – or so we're told. In that case, what was the reason for this?

Never, before or since, have I been so cut to the very core of my being. But somehow I carried on – people do. In time I realised that I wasn't the only one who had suffered in this way. So many devastating things happen to people. Just the other day I read in the newspaper about a mother losing her three children in a house fire. Her grief is beyond my imagination. Other people's losses don't make it any easier at the time and nothing can replace the person who's gone. But you do mature into an appreciation of the good things in your life that some people never experience. I was very struck by something Richard Nixon was once reported as saying. Only someone who's been in the deepest valley, he said, can know what it means to stand on the highest mountain; and whether he was a good or a bad man, that has always struck me as very true. I couldn't have known then the extraordinary turn of events my professional life would take all those years later, or the enduring love I would find in my personal life in my thirties. But President Nixon was right. To appreciate the highs, you need to have known the lows.

I still talk to my son. The deep sadness doesn't go away. He'd be in his early forties now, which seems incredible to imagine. I returned to work a couple of weeks after his premature birth. I had no parents I could rely on and no man to support me, financially or in any other way. Carrying on wasn't a matter of choice: I had no alternative. If I didn't work I wouldn't get paid, simple as that; and no one else was going to pay my rent. But it was to take a long time before I would come up for air, and the air would never again smell as nice and fresh as it had before.

I never saw John again until one day, about twenty years later, he drove past me in Formby and stopped to have a chat: he seemed a bit embarrassed. I nearly fainted, and I don't really know why he bothered. I was designing knitwear at the time and he'd seen me talking about my designs on the daytime television show *Pebble Mill at One*, where they were put on models and accessorised by Jeff Banks. He and Anne had married. Just before he got back in his car, he asked if I'd like to have lunch with him one day. I looked at him. 'I don't think so,' I said. I haven't seen him from that day to this, but I hope he and his wife are still together and happy. I wish them no ill.

You never forget, though. The events of the night of 22 February 1966 are forever etched on my memory. Sadly, although by choice, I never had a family of my own. What happened in that top-floor flat on Brompton Avenue partly explains my decision to remain childless. But my own childhood has never ceased to cast its shadow. If I'd had a child of my own I would have swamped it with material possessions, suffocated it with all the love I never knew. I know I'd have over-compensated for everything that had been missing from my own childhood. I'd have been far too indulgent, far too protective. In my own way I too would have produced a deranged human being.

Back in 1966, I moved out of Brompton Avenue as soon as I could find somewhere else to live. I couldn't stay there because it held too many painful memories. So I answered an ad in the local paper and got myself a lovely bedsit in Ivanhoe Road, not far away in Liverpool 15. It was kept beautifully by the landlady, Mrs Wright, who lived on the premises but at the back of the house which meant I had my privacy. Her daughter lived there too: she was at drama school and went on to become a professional actress with the stage name of Cheryl Murray. Her most famous role was as Suzie Birchall in *Coronation Street*, in which she appeared for seven years from 1977.

I too changed my name. I wanted to be a different person altogether. I'd liked the look of the actress

Kim Novak in a film I'd seen, and I liked her first name. Nobody could shorten it. Also, I'd never cared for the name Pat. Quite apart from the fact that it reminded me of my mother, I'd always thought it sounded like an Irish navvy. This was going to be a turning point for me. I was leaving behind me my sad, lonely childhood, dominated by that brutal woman. I was going to move on from the wretched night when I'd lost my baby boy. Now I was Kim. I was looking forward.

12

A New Beginning

That never-to-be-forgotten night brought about many changes: a change of name, a change of home and, quite quickly afterwards, a change of employment. I lost the appetite for standing up in department stores selling perfume and cosmetics, and I was never going to miss the commuting at either end of the day. I decided I'd look for a job nearer home where I'd be surrounded by people, and I got one in a pub. Now I'd be too busy to dwell on what had happened, and tired enough at the end of the day to get some much-needed sleep.

The Hanover House in Hanover Street, right in the heart of Liverpool, was a lovely, oak-beamed pub that was always full. All that was required of me was that I should have a smile on my face and a nice word for all the customers. There was no hanging around, and no conversation was ever going to last more than a couple of minutes. And financially I was better off, because I was getting good tips on top of my wages. In my time off I went clubbing or on the odd date – there was no one special in my life – or out for a meal with friends. But despite the busy job and the active social life I'd wake up almost every night with my head full of everything that had happened. I was so unhappy, and not really able to share it with anyone else.

For a couple of years, I deliberately filled my life with as much activity as possible. I lived in a whirlwind as I continued to try to suppress all thoughts of my past. Then one day I woke up and asked myself a question. If I died tomorrow, what would I be sorry I hadn't done? And I knew the answer straightaway. I'd be sorry I hadn't gone to drama school. Whether it was appearing in the Brownies' nativity play, dreaming of Hollywood stardom as I read celebrity magazines, making a little money at modelling or even using my personality to sell products in stores around the country, I knew there was something of a thwarted performer in me. Perhaps I ought to see if I really did have any talent before I left it too late.

Cheryl, my landlady's daughter, was ten years younger than me and had recently enrolled at the Elliot Clarke School of Dance and Drama in Bold Street. Chatting to her mother one day, I told her of my ambition and Mrs Wright suggested I try for a place and maybe I'd be given a grant as a mature student. And that's exactly what happened. I passed my audition and had no trouble getting a grant. I worked full-time at the Hanover until term started in September, and after that did shifts there at weekends. Later on I left the Hanover altogether and worked at a nightclub on Friday and Saturday evenings; the wages and the tips were even better. I'd also saved some money by then, which helped to supplement my grant.

But still my past had an awkward habit of intruding. By the time his grandparents died in Sunderland, within months of each other, my half-brother Richard – second son of my mother and Mac – was nineteen. He'd been born while Gloria and I were shut away in Nazareth House at the mercy of those cold-hearted nuns, and then taken up north when he was just three months old. With the couple who had raised him now gone Richard was keen to track down his birth parents, but he had no idea how to find them. So he advertised in newspapers all over the country. And when I picked up a local Liverpool paper one day I read that someone called Richard McGinley was looking for his parents.

I felt sure this was the brother I'd never met, so I rang the newspaper and they gave me a contact number. When I got in touch with Richard and explained that I thought I was his half-sister he said he hadn't known I existed. We arranged to meet in London, where he was now living in lodgings in Shepherd's Bush. When we did meet up I was struck by the fact that he looked very much like another half-brother, Neil. He wasn't as friendly as I'd hoped, although we chatted for a long time. He looked to me like a boy who had the weight of the world on his shoulders.

In the end, and although I only had my modest little place back in Liverpool, I offered him a bed there while he got himself sorted out. But he turned me down because, he said, he wanted to track down his mother and father. I told him a little about my unhappy family life and explained that I was pretty sure my mother and Mac were still in the Portsmouth area, but that I had no idea where they lived or whether they were even still together. I didn't try to put him off finding them. He was an adult and it was his business what he did with his life. I never saw him or heard from him again for fifteen years, until I took my second husband to meet my mother in Portsmouth and found Richard living with her.

As it turned out, my mother's younger sister Teresa – known as Terry – had seen Richard's advert in a Portsmouth paper and told my mother.

I've never known Terry very well. Twelve years older than me, she married very young and raised three children with her late husband, Stan. She and my mother had been quite close when they were growing up – they were the only girls among five children – but they'd gradually grown apart. Like everyone else, she knew my mother was trouble and so kept clear. But Terry must have been curious to know whether this Richard McGinley was my mother's son by Mac because she wouldn't otherwise have got in touch with her.

By then, as I later discovered, Mac and my mother were living in Westfield Road, just round the corner from Suffolk Road. She got in touch with Richard, and that's how he eventually came to move in with them. No one could have predicted it at the start, but Richard's arrival finally signalled the end of my mother's long-running affair with Mac. My mother and Richard became close to the point where Mac, now in his late forties, obviously felt he'd been relegated to second-best; so he moved out, and never came back. He went to live in the most dismal little bedsit in a house somewhere in Portsmouth. Uncle Neville visited him there on more than one occasion, and said it was sad to see him in such reduced circumstances. Not that he did much more than sleep there – he'd work all day and spend all evening in the pub. But he still gave my mother twelve pounds ten shillings, a huge chunk of his wages, a week to help with the children.

Back in Liverpool I now saw much less of Michael and Sally – I associated them too much with my unhappy past – although she and I would sometimes meet up. One day in June 1969 I was walking with her along Lodge Lane, not far from where I lived. Suddenly, a car started slowing down and drew to a halt right by us. I didn't know it at the time, but it was an unmarked police car. The two men inside told us they were constables in the CID, but it became quickly clear that they weren't on police business. The one at the wheel was called Stan; the one leaning out of the window was Ken. 'Hello, ladies,' he said. 'Are you going our way?' It was broad daylight with lots of traffic around, so we accepted a lift.

I was instantly attracted to Ken. He had a look of Burt Reynolds about him – tall and slim, with a muscular figure. He'd been fat as a boy – later on, he showed me some childhood photographs – but he'd been given such a rough time by the other kids at school that he'd vowed never to be fat again. His dark hair was cut in a Beatle fringe, which was the fashion then, and he was quite a sharp dresser – a bit on the spivvy side, I now think as I look back. He was a buck, and the women loved him. And he had the most beautiful, rich, dark brown speaking voice. He was also very adept at seduction. One of his ploys was to write a succession of love poems which he'd dedicate to whoever he was pursuing.

A few days later he was at my front door – he'd made a note of where I lived when he and Stan dropped me off. By the time September came round I'd started at drama school and Ken and I were an item. We'd quickly become lovers; there was a very strong mutual attraction. But we weren't doing anyone any harm. We were both single – or so I thought. He seemed to be able to see me whenever he wanted. I later learned that the men in the CID could come and go pretty much as they pleased. They might be up all night, asleep half the day. They were more or less their own bosses and hard to keep tabs on. That suited Ken.

I was falling deeply in love with this man, and my feelings for him put into perspective what I'd felt for John before the trauma of losing my baby. That relationship now seemed more like puppy love. At the time I'd been happy to find someone who seemed to care for me, because that was such an unusual occurrence in my life. But I quickly realised that what I felt for Ken was on a completely different, deeper plane. Our sex life was active although Ken wasn't an especially good lover – much keener on his own enjoyment than on mine – but I was so attracted to him that I didn't care. And he never stopped telling me how much he loved me. Everything was swinging along fine. Then he turned up one day, about six weeks into our relationship, with a ring on his wedding finger. It stopped me dead in my tracks. He told me not to be so silly. It was his great-grandmother's, he said, and he wore it if the fancy took him.

That was nonsense, of course, and in my heart of hearts I knew it. A couple of weeks later, I looked him in the eye. 'You're a very attractive man, you know,' I said. 'How come you didn't have a girlfriend when we first met? Are you sure you're not married?'

It was as though he couldn't be bothered with the pretence any longer. 'All right,' he admitted, 'I *am* married. But if I'd told you that when we first met, you wouldn't have gone out with me. And, without a shadow of a doubt, you are the love of my life.'

I was terribly shocked but I'd fallen in love with him by then. What was I supposed to do?

He added, 'And I can't part from you. I just can't.'

He'd been married three years to a woman called Joan, although they'd been together longer than that. They'd met when they were young. The story he gave me was that, in all their courtship, they'd never slept together. She'd point-blank refused, telling him she wanted to be a virgin on her wedding night. 'In the end,' said Ken, 'I married her to get her body.' It was only after he'd got a ring on her finger that he realised he'd made a big mistake. Their sex life was dreadful, he said; he wished he'd slept with her before they got married; and so on . . . I'd never have got involved with him if I'd known all this, but it was too late now.

Ken said his wife knew something was wrong with the marriage and he was going to tell her about me – and then we'd get married. That, at least, is the line he spun me. I later discovered that his wife was absolutely broken-hearted when she found out about me. Joan thought they had a good marriage. She'd had no idea Ken was being unfaithful to her; and there had been other women before me. Ken had told me so himself.

He and I were sitting in my bedsit in Ivanhoe Road one day when suddenly we heard a commotion on the stairs and two men started hammering on my door. It was Joan's twin brother Chris and a friend, and they weren't happy. They were threatening to lay into Ken for what he'd done to Joan.

'You fucking bastard!' Chris shouted. 'You've treated my Joan like dirt for years. You've knocked her about but she's kept it secret. If she'd told me, I'd have killed you years ago.'

I couldn't believe what I was hearing. Ken might have been a ladies' man, but surely he wouldn't hit a woman? I saw Joan once when I went with Ken to pick up something from his house. She was a tiny blonde. Ken was a policeman. Could he really have stooped so low as to assault a small, defenceless woman?

And then I remembered something he'd said in an unguarded moment a couple of months earlier. Although he spent most of his time with me, he'd occasionally pop home for a shower and a change of clothes. On one occasion he got back to Ivanhoe Road and said, 'Bloody hell! I was minding my own business when Joan and her mother walked in. She always brings that woman with her.'

I don't think he realised what he was saying. I asked him, 'Why would she always want her mother with her?'

He didn't hesitate. 'Well, Joan tells her mother that I hit her. She's frightened to be on her own with me.'

I said, 'You don't, do you?'

He looked genuinely horrified. 'Of course not,' he replied. 'What do you think I am?'

I should have taken more notice of that little conversation and what her twin brother had said. Joan had reason to be frightened – as I was to find out to my cost.

When Joan's brother finally left my bedsit, Ken told me to take no notice of what he'd been saying. He'd never laid a finger on Joan. Her brother was only talking in that wild way because he didn't like to see his sister upset over her broken marriage. I wasn't quite sure what to think. This was the man I loved and the man who loved me. And the trouble with love is that it's deaf and blind. Ken said I was the woman of his dreams and that he was divorcing Joan. She'd now gone back to live with her mother and Ken wouldn't rest, he said, until he'd made me his wife.

In the meantime, I'd started at drama school – at twenty-seven, I was the oldest student there. To begin with at least, it was a laugh. Quite quickly, however, I realised the course wasn't up to much. The principal, Sheilagh Elliot Clarke, was a cross between Margaret Rutherford and James Robertson Justice. She might have been good at her job and so might her deputy, but neither of them ever seemed to be around. Sheilagh was meant to take our class three afternoons a week, but as often as not she'd get her favourite student, a seventeen-year-old called Lorraine Gould, to stand in for her. Then Sheilagh developed a bad chest and she gave up teaching altogether.

I hadn't got a grant or saved up my hard-earned wages to be taught by a teenager, so I complained.

'How dare you!' she boomed.

But, as I told her, at twenty-seven I wasn't going to get this opportunity again. I certainly wouldn't be given another grant.

My complaint fell on deaf ears, though, and that left me with a straightforward choice: I could leave the drama school there and then, although I didn't fancy the idea of returning to shop work, or I could relax and enjoy myself. We were being taught next to nothing, but the other students were a laugh. I was going out with Ken, a good-looking man who'd left his marriage for me and was my first great love. Life could be worse, I reckoned.

Oh yes it could. I might have thought I hadn't a care in the world, but the one person guaranteed to bring me back down to earth was about to make a reappearance in my life. A bunch of us were mucking around one afternoon at college when the phone rang. Sean Birks the student who was nearest picked it up and called across to me: 'It's for you – it's your mum.'

I felt like I'd been slapped round the face. 'Don't talk wet!' I answered. But I could see he wasn't joking. I must have turned deathly white because everyone in the room had stopped what they were doing to watch me walk towards the phone. My mother and I hadn't spoken in more than eleven years. How on earth had she tracked me down? I still kept in touch with my Uncle Neville. Perhaps he'd innocently mentioned to a member of the family that I was now at drama school and it had somehow got back to my mother. Armed with that information, and knowing I'd moved to Liverpool with my father, it wouldn't have taken her long to track me down.

By the time I picked up the receiver my blood had run cold.

'Hello,' she said. I'd have known that voice anywhere. 'How are you?'

I was immediately suspicious. 'What do you want?' I asked.

'That's a nice way to talk to your mother,' she replied. I told her she could stop right there – I knew this woman too well. 'One, you never were a mother to me. And two, you're obviously after something.'

She pretended to be very offended. 'I've just been wondering how you were,' she said.

No, she hadn't. 'You're after money,' I told her, and I could tell by the pause that followed that I'd hit the nail on the head. 'Well, I haven't got any, and if I had I wouldn't give it to you.' And then I put the phone down. She'd completely unnerved me. I looked down at my hands – they were trembling like leaves. After all that time, my mother could still do that to me.

It took me the rest of the day to recover from that nasty shock, and I thanked the stars above that I now had someone in my life who loved me with a passion. The only trouble was that Ken was becoming increasingly possessive. He hated me being at drama school. I can't say for sure why that was, but I think he was jealous – of the fun I was having without him, I suppose, and the fact that I was surrounded by lots of young people. There was to be a production of Oscar Wilde's *The Importance of Being Earnest* and I was cast as Lady Bracknell, complete with grey hair and long black gown. Sean Birks had told me that directors from Liverpool's prestigious Everyman Theatre often came to see these college productions to look for undiscovered talent. On the first night Ken was in the audience – the first person who'd ever come to see me in anything – with his policeman friend Stan. And Sean had been right: Ian Taylor, a bigwig from the Everyman, was in the audience too.

The play went well, and afterwards I was changing out of my costume into a tiny leather mini-skirt when Sean came bursting into my dressing room. Ian Taylor had asked if he could have a word with me. I couldn't get there fast enough. And he was so complimentary. 'You're very good, you know,' he said. 'You'll go far – although not at this school you won't. You'll pick up bad habits here that you'll never shake off. You need to get to London.' Then he told me he had good contacts at East 15, a highly respected drama school in London. There'd be no audition needed, he said; I'd be accepted on his recommendation. After I'd completed a full drama course there he'd give me a job at the Everyman.

This was the opportunity of a lifetime. I told Sean what Ian Taylor had said and his reaction was immediate. 'Oh, do it,' he said. 'You'd be mad not to.' And then I went over to Ken, who'd been waiting for me. Very quietly, I explained what had happened – and he gave me a look I'll never forget.

'I'm not having it,' he said. I just stared at him. Surely he couldn't deny me a chance like this? 'Look, I'll make it easy for you,' he said. 'If you go down to London, we're finished. It's one thing you being at drama school in Liverpool. But if you were based in London, we'd never see each other. And you'd never stay true to me. I can't have that – I'd worry all the time. You're the love of my life.'

If I'd known then what I know now, I'd have turned on my heel and headed straight for London. But I'd never been loved like this before and it made me feel I was being valued for myself and myself alone – that was something I'd never experienced. So I turned down Ian Taylor's offer and opted for love. I'd been at Elliot Clarke for just under a year – only half the course – but I'd had enough. The teaching wasn't what I expected, so I left. And since I'd also turned down the chance of being taught properly in London I reckoned I might as well give up the idea of being an actress – although, for my own pleasure, I paid for private lessons two nights a week at the Carnforth School of Dance and Drama in Allerton. And I must have been quite good at it, because in the end I gained nineteen diplomas for verse-speaking as well as winning the Elsie Webb Cup for character acting which was open to anyone in Liverpool. But this was all very much secondary to my personal life. I'd made my decision: I was throwing in my lot with Ken, committing myself to him. This was to be the start of a perfect long-term partnership.

But then the violence began. It was as though, having got me where he wanted, he relaxed and started showing his true colours. The ceiling of my bedsit in Ivanhoe Road curved at one point under the eaves. One evening Ken had been drinking and, for no reason that I can remember, lost his temper and charged at the curved ceiling. His head smashed right through it. That frightened me – not because he'd threatened me in any way but because it showed how irrationally, how violently, he could behave.

It wasn't long before I became the target. His attitude to the drama school had only been the beginning, and he proved to be insanely jealous of anything I did or anyone I spoke to: he had to be involved. It took me a little while to understand this, but Ken needed to be in absolute control. He was the youngest of five children whose parents had scraped together the money to give them a good education. His father had started sweeping the floor of his local Co-op at fourteen and had gradually worked his way up to manager. Ken's eldest brother, Tom, was Chief Superintendent of the CID in Southport. His sister, Lily, was a head midwife who ran one wing of a hospital in Yorkshire. His twin brothers, Edward and James, were a lecturer at Quebec University and a sea captain respectively.

And then there was Ken, who was just a constable. His parents had paid for him to go to Conway Sea School, after which he became a midshipman. But he was only interested in having a good time, and hadn't stuck at it. He was, therefore, the black sheep of the family. His brother Tom once told me he thought Ken might be schizophrenic – and I think he was right. If I popped out to get a loaf of bread from the corner shop there was hell to pay. 'I could have brought that in!' he'd shout. What did he imagine I'd be doing between the house and the shop? Like my mother, he could lose his temper over nothing – we'd be talking perfectly normally and he'd suddenly flare up.

The first time he punched me – full in the face – we'd been talking about getting married. 'But we haven't known each other that long,' I said. 'We don't have to rush.'

He glared at me. 'We're in love, aren't we?'

I replied that we knew we were, but we could take our time.

'Why?' he demanded. 'Have you got somebody else?'

I looked at him. 'Oh, Ken,' I said, 'of course I haven't. Anyway, I never go anywhere without you by my side.'

And that's when he lashed out. I should have thrown him out at that very moment and never allowed him back. But he was quickly full of remorse. 'It's only because I love you so much,' he said. And, fool that I was, I believed him.

Most of the time he was passive and quiet; but then he would hit top C without warning. For example, before we bought an apartment in Gateacre, a well-to-do suburb in south Liverpool, we lived briefly in a rented flat in Allerton. Living with her boyfriend in the same block was a girl called Christine who worked with me at Lewis's. Many years later I bumped into her in the street and she told me that one day Ken had knocked on their front door because he'd seen the boyfriend through the window. The man had come to the door. 'I've seen you staring at my girlfriend,' Ken had accused him. 'If I ever catch you doing that again, I'll fucking flatten you.'

I used to shop in Hargreaves, a local supermarket in Allerton, but I was never allowed to go there alone. One day, Ken and I turned up there together. As we approached the bacon counter he told me to stand to one side, and then walked up to the men who worked behind the counter. 'If I catch any of you fuckers looking at my wife,' he said menacingly, 'you'll none of you have a fucking job.'

When we got home, I told him I'd never so much as noticed any of the guys in the supermarket. In which case, he replied, why were they looking at me like that? And then he lashed out with his open hand. He'd always slap me on the face or punch me with a closed fist. Sometimes he'd pin my arm right up my back until I cried out with pain, or he'd knock me across the room.

His possessiveness, which now bordered on insanity, was the reason I never suspected he was two-timing me. It's also why I went on to marry him. I believed that this man, warts and all, really adored me, and that was such an amazing new experience. He was so devoted to me that sometimes, or so I reasoned, his passion would spill over into violence. Stupid, I know, but to me even the bad times were good. On one occasion, after a particularly nasty row when I'd threatened to walk out, he threw me on the floor, straddled me and put his hands round my throat. 'Say that ever again,' he growled, 'and I'll fucking kill you. You're never going to fucking leave me.' All the love I'd never known was somehow concentrated in this intensely passionate man.

On Saturday, 10 July 1971, at eleven o'clock in the morning and just over two years after we'd first met, Ken and I were married in a registry office in Brougham Terrace in Liverpool. His sister Lily and her gynaecologist boyfriend were our only witnesses. I was twenty-nine. I wore a polyester dress and matching coat in pale grey. My hair was arranged in loads of curls, the fashion at the time. Ken wore a plain dark grey suit. It was a very short service. Even at the time, I remember wondering if I was doing the right thing. We'd rowed and fought throughout the previous evening. But on the day itself he couldn't have been more demonstrative, showering me with love and more of his poems.

After the ceremony, just the two of us went for a meal in a local Indian restaurant. There wasn't any question of a honeymoon – Ken didn't want to travel. In the six years we were together we never went abroad or even out of Liverpool, come to that. All he ever wanted to do was drink and smoke and, as I was soon to find out, sleep with as many women as possible. And his job gave him the perfect licence to do just that. He'd raid clubs and then meet all these girls. He could tell me he was doing one thing, and then be doing something quite different. We'd walk around Liverpool and he seemed to know half the pretty girls we bumped into. That was because he was in the CID, he said; it was his business to know what was going on. But I needn't worry. I was the love of his life.

I needed a job and got taken on as manageress of a medium-sized fashion store called Finnegan's in the centre of Liverpool, opposite the Hanover pub. I had a staff of thirty. It had been a family-run business but had recently been taken over. The previous manageress, a Mrs Radcliffe, was still working there. She was much older than me and I'd have understood if she'd resented me being appointed over her. But Radi, as she was known, was a lovely woman, full of kindness and wisdom – two qualities that were to prove invaluable in the months to come.

Ken would drop in if he was passing and all the assistants thought he was great: he drew women to him like a magnet. He was the strong, silent type who liked to make women feel sorry for him. At Ivanhoe Road, most of the rooms were taken by nurses. Sometimes when we were living there before we married, we'd all get together for a drink. The nurses had nicknamed him Soulful Face, and Ken played up to that. Like my mother before him, he was always putting on an act. What nobody saw – including me at first – was his other side, the face of a bully.

By the Christmas of 1973, just eighteen months into the marriage, Ken had turned into a different person. He'd grown more and more distant to me and stayed out all hours. In the early days of our relationship, when I was living in Ivanhoe Road, he'd seemed to be able to get off work an hour or two early; it was referred to as taking an early dart. I'd be lying in bed and suddenly I'd hear a pebble hit the window. I'd look out and there would be Ken. It was very romantic.

But since our marriage there'd been no early darts – or that's what he told me. In just a year and a half our sex life had dwindled to little or nothing. And yet I'd get in from work and he'd want to know why I was five minutes late; his jealousy hadn't diminished at all. He'd think nothing of hitting me or kicking me when his temper suddenly flared; and nowadays he showed no remorse afterwards. His explanation, if he ever offered one, was that he loved me too much and couldn't bear the thought of us not being together. So, despite knowing that he'd cheated on Joan, it never crossed my mind that he might be cheating on me.

The neighbours downstairs, an elderly couple, had started complaining to the police about Ken coming home drunk and shouting and knocking me about. But he was one of theirs, so they always covered for him. And he was very crafty about keeping in with the right people. He knew a lot of their secrets so that, while he wasn't popular, as I was later to discover, he was feared.

At work, Radi had originally urged me to patch up my marriage, to work hard at saving it. But she was worried, she said, by Ken's increasing violence – although she found it hard to reconcile with his other actions. Most days he'd pop into the shop and seem so attentive to me. And I'd tell her of the many occasions he broke down in front of me in tears, pleading with me never to cheat on him. 'I'd die without you,' he'd say.

The man seemed totally besotted with me, almost literally madly in love. He'd tell me of the countless times, as a uniformed bobby, he'd seen me near where I lived. He'd lacked the confidence back then, he said, to start a conversation with me. He'd thought I was out of his league. There was a

Stevie Wonder song, 'My Cherie Amour', that was popular at the time and concerned a man's unattainable love for a woman. Ken told me that he really identified with the lyric: 'How I wish that you were mine.' When he and I got together, it became 'our' song.

Ken continued to write a lot of poetry and, I must admit he was quite good. I even got one of them published in a poetry book. There's one particular poem which I can still recite from memory:

Some spend their life seeking places
On that golden piece of earth
That shows in old, old faces
In lines of laughter and mirth

Some seek forever and always
All over life's bitter grey land
For all life's turns and pathways
But joy is so seldom at hand

The few may eventually find it
The joy when life is complete
But the secret is just to keep it
Through lies and utter deceit

The rest just go fumbling onwards
Not knowing where real happiness may be

They take the place of a coward
When life's loud voice makes its plea

Happiness is made by giving
Of oneself to another in need
Self-love is the wrong kind of living
And brings only sorrow and greed

It was staring me in the face, but what I couldn't see at the time was the poem's all-too-plain coded message. Ken clearly intended to live a life of lies and deceit. He'd said as much in verse. That was his way of finding happiness. I read that poem again after we divorced and its message couldn't have been more obvious. But by then, of course, the damage had been done.

13

Lies, Deceit, Betrayal

By 1974, I was no longer able to avoid the uncomfortable truth. Having pursued me with all the charm and flattery he could muster and having made me fall head over heels for him, my husband no longer wanted me. If I'd only had ears to hear it five years earlier, it was precisely the pattern he'd established with his first wife. Wasn't it Ken himself who'd told me that he'd married Joan to get her into bed? And then when he'd had her, he didn't want her any more. Here was a man who loved the chase but who got bored once he'd bagged the prey.

He was rarely home at our flat in Gateacre when I was around, but I remember clearly one evening when he was sitting in a towelling robe in front of the television watching his beloved Bill Shankly, legendary manager of Liverpool Football Club. I wasn't happy. All those familiar feelings of loneliness had come flooding back. I felt unloved and rejected. I walked into the room and said, 'Look, Ken, we need to talk.'

He waved me away. 'I'm watching the fucking football.'

But I persisted. 'Ken,' I repeated, 'we need to talk about *us*. There's something wrong here. We've barely been married three years. But we hardly ever have sex. You're never home. You never seem to get early darts any more – or so you claim. And yet I can't even go to the shops without you creating blue murder. What's going on?'

Instead of answering me he lifted his robe, turned on his side, pointed his bare backside at me and broke wind in my face. How much more insulting could he be? I walked straight into our bedroom, packed my bags and took off my wedding ring, which I left by the bed. Then I checked into the Feathers, a small bed and breakfast in the centre of Liverpool and just a walk from Finnegan's where I still worked as manageress. I didn't think at the time I was turning my back on my marriage; I couldn't believe that the depths of what we had once felt for each other had disappeared for ever. But I very much wanted to show my husband that I meant business. I was sure it would bring him to his senses.

I'd been gone three days when I got a phone call from Ken at the shop. My absence had clearly made him keener because it was 'darling' this and 'darling' that.

'What's happened to us?' he said. 'Where did we go wrong? I love you so much. If anything ever happened to you, my world would come to an end.'

But I wasn't falling for it.

Then he asked, 'Are you coming home?'

I couldn't see the point.

'But I love you.'

'In which case,' I replied, 'you've got a funny way of showing it.'

There was a pause. 'So you're not coming back?'

I told him I wanted to stay away for a few more days and then see how I felt.

'Fine,' he said, 'but as soon as you've made up your mind, please tell me when you're coming home. I'll come and pick you up from the shop.' And with that he put down the phone.

This was a man who was full of contradictions. He hardly ever came near me, and yet here he was swearing his undying devotion. I wanted to believe him. I wasn't about to throw away my marriage – not after all the happiness we'd known together. My existence before Ken had been all about survival, but he'd shown me that life could be wonderful. Yes, we'd been having problems – but I'd moved out and now he seemed to be coming to his senses. Maybe I should take him at his word. Maybe, cutting through all his nonsense, Ken really did still love me.

I'd already got into the habit of confiding in Radi at work. I told her that beneath all the violence and screaming matches, beneath the indifference he'd shown me the night I left, perhaps Ken really did have feelings for me. Radi, wise old owl, would arch an eyebrow. His violence towards me was all wrong and she let me know it. But at least there was no other woman involved and I was still very much in love with him. It was hard to fathom the man although, as the days went on, I began to feel there was good reason to be hopeful. If he wasn't interested in whether I returned home or not, why would he have bothered to ring to find out my intentions? I had my answer soon enough – but it was the last thing I wanted to discover.

A week later, I made up my mind to go home and sort out my life. I didn't call Ken but booked a taxi instead. I got indoors at about quarter past seven. He wasn't there, but I was sure he'd be back sooner or later. I looked round the flat; it badly needed to be cleaned and tidied. I wasn't surprised. Ken wouldn't have done any of that, living there alone. And perhaps he'd been pining for me – or that's what I told myself. I waited and waited. Still no Ken. So I rang the police station and asked if he was on duty that evening. No, I was told. Then the man on the other end of the phone asked who was calling. I said I was Ken's wife. 'Oh,' he said quickly. 'He might be working – I'm really not sure.' I could tell the man was covering for him.

I sat there until eleven o'clock, which seemed an eternity. What on earth was going on? In the end I grew restless and decided to go outside to see if I could spot him coming home. I let myself out of our front door and as I got to the street – our flat was on the first floor – I saw two figures coming towards me in the dark: Ken and a young girl. I later discovered that she was called Valerie and had just turned seventeen, which meant she was almost half Ken's age. Confronted by me on the path leading to our apartment block, my husband took one look and 'Jesus Christ!' he groaned. 'No chance.' What he meant was that I'd caught him totally and utterly red-handed. The pair of them turned on their heels, hurried to Ken's car and drove off.

I was so shocked that my teeth were chattering. I went back up to the flat and sat down. Even though he'd behaved so badly over the previous year, I'd never for a moment thought he was cheating on me. I got up, marched into the bedroom and pulled back the bedclothes. The sheets were covered in semen stains. So not only had Ken been sleeping with a girl young enough to be his daughter, he'd been doing it in our bed. Then it hit me like a thunderbolt. Of course! That's why he'd wanted to know when I was coming home. It had nothing to do with his professed undying love for me. It had everything to do with checking that the coast was clear for him to bring Val into our flat, into our bed.

It was then that I realised my wedding ring had gone. Had Ken put it somewhere for safe keeping? Who knows? I changed the sheets and got into bed, but I couldn't sleep. I knew my marriage was over. I'm the sort of person who could never get over a man cheating on me with another woman. Ken had seemed to me to be the first man, the first *person* ever in my life to have loved me unconditionally. And yet once again I'd been let down. Was I doomed never to find lasting happiness?

At six o'clock the next morning I heard the key in the lock. Ken was back, this time alone. He walked straight up to me and looked me in the eye. 'Kim,' he told me, 'it's not what you think.'

I said, 'Ken, you've broken my heart. Don't add more lies to everything else you've done. I saw the sheets on our bed. I want a divorce. Please, no more lies. The least you owe me is the truth.' And I asked about Val. It turned out that she'd been thrown out of the family home because she'd been running wild all over Liverpool 8. She was out of control, and she'd turned up at the police station because her parents wouldn't allow her back. Ken volunteered to take her to talk to them.

I didn't know whether this revelation was meant to gain my sympathy, but if so it didn't work. Instead of trying to steer her back on to the straight and narrow he'd taken an impressionable girl – she was only sixteen at the time – into his bed. She must have been very flattered. 'I thought I could show her the better things in life,' he said. The man was self-deluded. Ken her saviour? Who was he kidding? Anyway, there was also the small matter of his unsuspecting wife sitting alone at home. I told him I honestly believed he should lose his job for the way he'd behaved and for the way he'd betrayed the trust of that girl's parents.

He hung his head. 'Kim,' he said, 'I'll never see her again. You're the one I love.'

But I'm afraid I wasn't going to be won over. I'd seen the sheets. 'Ken, I could never trust you again. I'm putting the flat up for sale.' Then a thought struck me. 'Oh, and by the way, what happened to my wedding ring?'

He tried to change the subject, so I repeated the question. 'I gave it to Val,' he said. The ultimate betrayal! He knew it from the look on my face. Then he walked out of the flat and, I thought, out of my life. But within the hour he was back again. 'Here's your ring,' he said. I told him he could put it on the table. Then he begged me not to leave him, begged me not to put the flat on the market. But my mind was made up. I'd been let down so many times in my life. I knew I couldn't stay with this man. It was over.

But he wouldn't move out. We had a joint mortgage, although he made all the payments via direct debit from his bank account, so he was entitled to live there. But I made him sleep in the spare bedroom – he and I never shared a bed again. It was a horrible period in my life and it lasted much longer than it might have done. If I'd known then how long Ken and I would have to continue to live like that I'd have found myself a bedsit. It was a nice flat, but the housing market was depressed and it took ages to sell.

Ken claimed he wasn't seeing Val any more. But I didn't believe him. He arrived back one evening very late – it must have been two in the morning – and he'd been drinking. I accused him of having been with that girl.

'No, I fucking haven't,' he said, and then punched me in the face.

Life was intolerable. It seems ridiculous to me now that I opted to stay in the same flat as a two-timing thug. But I was very confused. I knew my marriage was over and I knew that Ken had behaved unforgivably – and yet this had been the great love affair of my life and I found it difficult simply to shut the door on it. My feelings for him ran very deep and I couldn't just brush them aside.

It never entered my head to try and woo him back, but something was preventing me from walking out of that flat and going to live on my own again. It would represent such an admission of failure, and I just wasn't strong enough to deal with that. My self-esteem had been fragile enough until I'd met Ken. His love for me had given me a confidence I'd never known – and now he didn't want me any more. It was a crushing blow and, as so often before, I was exhibiting physical signs of the stress I was under. My hair had started falling out again so I went to the doctor, who diagnosed alopecia areata as a nervous reaction to all the sadness and turmoil.

I was also trying to drown my sorrows – not that drink ever manages to do that. I'd sit alone in the flat each evening, knocking back whisky or Drambuie. At work, Radi was effectively carrying me – she was so good to me. I'd drink there, too. I had a Little Red Riding Hood-type basket that I took with me to Finnegan's every day, and I always made sure it contained some bottles of alcohol. I wasn't coping with life in any way, shape or form.

One day when I turned up Radi looked at me and said, 'You know, that man is killing you. I'm watching you go down and down. Just look at you. You're fading away to nothing.' She was right. The weight was dropping off me – but then I wasn't eating properly.

The months went by and we were still stuck in the flat together. Ken had given up trying to persuade me to change my mind and take him back, and anyway I don't believe that was what he really wanted. He never once tried to climb into the bed we used to share. On the other hand, he showed no remorse for the way he'd destroyed our marriage. In fact he used to flaunt his womanising in my face if we were ever at home together. He'd think nothing of strolling around the flat with just a towel wrapped round his middle, taking pleasure in the love bites he was displaying – all round his nipples and his navel, and all over his shoulders. It disgusted me. But I never let him know that I'd noticed. He'd try to provoke me. 'See,' he'd say, pointing to the love bites. 'You may not care but she does.' But I wasn't going to play that game.

It was the spring of 1975 – with the flat still not sold – when Ken returned one night, drunk as usual. The next morning, bleary-eyed, he started strutting around in a skimpy pair of underpants. He was fond of preening himself in front of the mirror, and then he'd karate-chop his stomach hard as if to show how flat it was and what good condition he was in. But there was something about his attitude that particular morning that frightened me. I sensed that he was playing with me, waiting for the moment when he could torture me with some new revelation.

I didn't have to wait long. Slowly, he turned to me. 'Oh, by the way,' he said, 'I thought you ought to know. I've got venereal disease.'

My mouth fell open.

'I've had it before,' he said. 'I know what it looks like. There's a discharge from the end of my penis.' It was almost as though he was proud of what he was saying.

I just stared at him. Did this mean I might have it, too? And yet we hadn't slept together in months.

It was as though he was reading my thoughts. 'Oh,' he added, 'and you might want to get yourself checked out.'

Suddenly, I was full of fear. Was a sexually transmitted disease to be the only legacy of my marriage? I began to sob quietly, thinking my life couldn't get any worse.

Ken's mood instantly changed, and he came and sat beside me. 'If only we could start again,' he said. 'I love you and I know you love me.'

It felt as if he was deliberately twisting a knife

into my heart, but it was sufficient to produce a spark of anger in me. 'Yes, I do still love you, Ken,' I said, 'very much indeed. But I wouldn't take you back now if you were the last man on God's earth.'

Might I really have venereal disease? To be on the safe side I decided to call my doctor. He said he was almost certain I wouldn't have been affected, given the length of time that had elapsed since I'd last had sex with Ken. But it wouldn't do any harm to be absolutely sure. Women could carry the disease for some time without knowing it, he told me; with men, it becomes apparent in a matter of days. I said I'd be too embarrassed to go to a VD clinic so the doctor recommended a specialist. That was going to cost me money I could ill afford, but I needed peace of mind. I told Ken what I was going to do and then suggested he got medical advice himself. That evening he went to see our GP and, when he got back to the flat he was full of mock indignation. 'I went to see the doctor,' he complained, 'and he was very rude to me.'

I told him I wasn't surprised and that I'd spoken to him earlier on the phone.

When Ken had said he thought he had VD, the doctor had apparently looked at him with open hostility. So Ken had unzipped his trousers and pulled his pants down. 'You can put that away,' the doctor had said, 'and you can get to a clinic. In the meantime, you can also get yourself out of my surgery.' Ken was a policeman, supposed to be a pillar of the community. Clearly, the doctor was utterly contemptuous of him.

Despite my protests Ken insisted on coming to the specialist with me. Was it guilt? Was he gloating? But I told him he had to wait outside. The specialist was very professional, although I wish he had been a woman. I had to put my feet in stirrups and then submit myself to an internal examination. Happily, he couldn't see any signs of anything bad; and he'd have the test results within a week, he said.

I was near to tears when I walked out into the street. No sign of Ken. After all he'd made me go through, he couldn't even be bothered to wait for me. I'd started walking towards the bus stop when suddenly I caught sight of him out of the corner of my eye. He was running towards me. When he drew level, he explained that he'd been to look round the ultra-modern Catholic cathedral that had just been built. Its nickname was the Mersey Funnel.

'Oh, it's lovely in there,' he exclaimed.

I looked hard at him. 'I'm glad you can see the beauty of the moment,' I replied.

If I'd imagined that Ken was trying to build bridges, I didn't have to wait long before I was brought to my senses once and for all. I'd complained to the police time and again about Ken's drunkenness and physical violence. As a result a panda car was often parked on the road outside our apartment block, in case he caused trouble when he got back and the neighbours complained. If ever a bobby knocked on the door when we were having a row or he was knocking me about, Ken wouldn't let him in. 'I know the law,' he'd shout. 'You can just fuck off.' And they did. To me, it was inconceivable that he kept his job because he'd broken pretty much every rule in the book; and yet his colleagues seemed keen to keep him out of trouble. But I don't think they cared too much, one way or the other, about me. Not, that is, until 3 July 1975.

I was in bed when Ken arrived home that night, but even from behind my closed door I could tell he was drunk – I could hear him bumping into the furniture. He'd obviously been out with Val; they'd patched things up by this stage. Suddenly my bedroom door was wrenched open, Ken walked in and in one movement he stripped off all the bedclothes. Then he stood at the end of the bed, fully clothed. I was naked and have never felt more vulnerable in my life, before or since.

'How are you,' he began, 'you fucking bitch?' He was swaying on his feet. 'What I ever saw in you I'll never know.'

I felt a mixture of revulsion, sadness and deep-seated fear. What was he going to do next?

He belched. 'Now,' he said, 'let's look at you, from top to bottom. You've got disgusting bald patches on your head. You've got freckles all over your body – which I find most unattractive. You've got a good nose – I'll grant you that – and nice eyes.' I'd been having electrolysis on the hairs on my chin; it's something most women have to deal with. Ken reached over and started fingering my face. I could smell the alcohol on his breath. 'Then there's your stubble,' he said. 'That's a real turn-off.'

He carried on down my body and started fondling my breasts. I'd have got up and walked out of the room there and then, but with him in this mood I thought it was wiser just to lie rigid on the bed. Was he about to rape me? I certainly wasn't going to do anything that might provoke him in any way.

'I will say this for you,' he continued. 'Your breasts may be big but they're quite firm. Val's half your age but her tits are already starting to sag.'

I was concentrating as hard as I knew how not to show him I was scared. I tensed my body to stop it trembling, but I could feel myself breaking into a sweat. Would Ken notice, and if so would he find that a turn-on?

'You've got a bit of a pot belly,' he went on. 'Still, no one can take this away from you – you've got great legs. Overall, though,' and he stepped back as if to consider my whole body, 'you're no gift.' And with that he flicked the bedclothes back over me and walked out of the room and into his own, slamming the door.

I thought I was going to be sick as my body began to shake uncontrollably. Ken hadn't physically abused me, but he might just as well have done. The mental cruelty and humiliation he'd just inflicted on me had been nothing less than barbaric. A line had been crossed. It was past midnight now, 4 July, Independence Day. And I thought, *I'm getting my independence from you, you bastard!* Once again anger replaced sadness, and I knew exactly what I was going to do next. I picked up the phone and rang the police station.

'Hello,' I said, 'this is Kim, Ken's wife, and I'm going to tell you something. I've rung you on numerous occasions to complain about my husband knocking me about, and you've never done anything. Well, I just reached the end of the road. If you don't take this man out of my house within the hour I'm going into his bedroom and I'm going to knife him. I promise you I'll kill him. I can't take it any more. Get him out, otherwise I won't be responsible for my actions.' And then I hung up.

Seven minutes later, four policemen were at my front door. I let them in and they opened the door to Ken's room. At the sight of them he broke down in tears, sobbing and sobbing, but it was too late. The bobbies told him to get his gear together and that he'd have to find somewhere to stay. He said he had a friend in Allerton who'd put him up. I told the police I didn't want to see any more of what was going on, then went into my bedroom and shut the door. When it sounded as though they might finally be taking Ken away, I came out and headed to the bathroom to splash some cold water on my face.

Then Ken appeared at the door and seemed to want something. He'd always been a vain man and spent ages in front of the mirror before he went out each day, combing his hair over a thinning patch on his crown. He'd also taken to rinsing his hair with a drop or two of Stergene – a laundry product – because he said it made the hair fluffier around the spot where it was going. He'd even resorted to putting brown boot polish on the back of his head. Amid all his tears and protestations of love for me, he'd asked his colleagues if he could beg just one more favour.

'Could I take the remains of that Stergene with me?' he asked.

I didn't know whether to laugh or cry. I handed him the bottle and then he was gone.

Five minutes later there was another knock on

the door. One of the policeman, a fat chap with a big stomach, was standing there as Ken lurked in the background. The bobby looked at me. 'Kim,' he said, 'all I can tell you is that this man loves you. He's been sobbing his heart out.' Ken didn't say anything.

'He loves me, does he?' I said. 'Well, for your information he's been sleeping with a teenage girl for the last year. He's an absolute pig. That man doesn't know what love is.'

And that's when Ken piped up. 'Do you know why you've lost me? It's because you're too kind. That's your downfall.'

I said, 'Go away, Ken.' And that was it.

Life was easier with Ken gone. I no longer dreaded the sound of the key in the lock. But I wasn't yet out of the wood. A month after he was led away by his fellow policemen I had to write out a cheque to settle a bill. Up until that point I hadn't touched a penny in our joint account. And yet the cheque bounced. So I rang the bank and told the clerk I knew there was about £900 in the account, quite a tidy sum in the mid-seventies.

He didn't beat about the bush. 'I'm sorry, madam,' he said. 'There's precisely one penny left in your account.' When I questioned this he said he'd put me on to the manager, and the man was quite short with me. Ken had removed all the money from the account with the exception of that one penny, he said, to keep it open – and, what's more, he'd been perfectly entitled to do so.

During our marriage, our habit had been to live off my weekly wage – I was paid in cash and it was kept in a wooden box in the flat – with Ken settling the mortgage and all the utility bills directly from his account. In fact he gave me just enough money each day from the box to pay for my lunch and bus fare to work. (But he never allowed me to travel home on public transport; that was when men were out and about who might ogle me, or so he maintained. So he'd always pick me up from work.) The morning after Ken had been forced to leave the flat, his heart apparently broken, a half-empty bottle of Stergene tucked under his arm, he'd gone to the bank and asked them to close the account. He was told that that would be impossible without my permission since I was the joint account holder. So he'd cleared out everything but one penny and I had no funds to meet the bills. Also, with Ken having cancelled the mortgage repayments the morning after the police had taken him away, the bank foreclosed on the flat which meant I wouldn't be able to live there any longer. Nor did I get any money from the eventual sale, because the proceeds were all absorbed by the outstanding loan. It was a terrible blow. I'd endured all those miserable months while we remained under the same roof, and now I didn't even have a penny to my name as I faced the uphill battle of starting out all over again.

I was not surprisingly feeling at my most vulnerable at this time, all my emotions only just below the surface, so what happened next was the last thing I needed. There were a couple of girls called Margie and Sonia whom I'd worked with on the bars at the nightclub, and occasionally I went out for an evening with them. Sonia had a boyfriend, a butcher called Bill, whom I met once, very briefly, when he was dropping off some meat at Margie's house. She had a car, she said, that she couldn't afford to get taxed and therefore couldn't park on the road. Could she leave it in my empty garage until she'd saved up enough money for the tax disc? In all innocence, I happily agreed.

About a week later she rang me at work and asked if Bill could drop in at the shop and pick up the keys. I didn't have them with me but, somewhat reluctantly, said he could come and borrow my front door key and get the garage keys from my empty flat. And still I didn't smell a rat. Bill showed up at the shop, but six hours later hadn't returned my front door key. I rang Sonia and asked her to chase him. She apologised, told me how forgetful he could be, and sure enough about half an hour before I was due to go home he reappeared with my key. I thought no more about it.

The following Friday Sonia, Margie and I were due to go out together, and Margie came round to my flat first for a coffee. We were sitting chatting when she suddenly said, 'Kim, did Sonia take you up on using your garage?'

I told her that Bill had come for my front door key and that I'd been a bit annoyed because he'd kept it for a good six hours.

She looked at me. 'I'd be very suspicious of that man,' she warned. 'He's a right villain – into everything. If I were you, I'd check that garage of yours. You want to make sure what's in there.'

My heart sank. She obviously knew something was up.

I got the key out of the drawer, went downstairs, unlocked the garage door – and nearly fainted on the spot. Up to the height of my chest and over the full length and breadth of the garage were hundreds and hundreds of untreated animal skins. That's when Margie told me that she'd heard on the radio about a big robbery from a warehouse in Litherland, five miles north of Liverpool. A big lorry containing thousands of animal skins awaiting export to be made into coats and so on had been stolen in the middle of the night. And there they were, sitting in my garage. Bill must have assumed

I wouldn't look in there, and he'd have been dead right if Margie hadn't alerted me. This was one more drama I had to deal with – and on my own.

But I didn't hesitate. I went straight back to the flat and rang the police. 'I don't know how to tell you this,' I said to the bobby on the other end of the phone, 'but I've got a garage full of untreated animal skins.' A fleet of police jeeps were outside the flat within minutes, and I told the man in charge the whole story. He asked where Sonia lived and I gave him her address. When they went to see her, she claimed to know nothing about the burglary. But, as they pointed out to her, she must have noticed that her boyfriend hadn't removed her car and put it in my garage because it was still sitting outside on the street. Even so, no charges were ever brought against her. But the police picked up Bill and his brother and they were both sent to prison.

I rang Sonia. 'How could you have done that to me?' I said. 'I was at my lowest ebb. You knew what I'd been going through.'

She protested her innocence but I told her I didn't believe her – and, anyway, what was Margie doing tipping me off?

I never saw either of them again and tried to concentrate on getting on with my life. But my future looked bleak and I'd lost so much confidence. I thought back to the days when Ken was wooing me and I was at drama school. Back then I had seemed a different person, happy and carefree I'd emerged from the long, dark tunnel of my loveless childhood. I'd somehow survived the terrible trauma of losing my darling son. At long last, the sun was beginning to shine on me. And yet it had all gone wrong. My husband had gone and I was on my own again, so much lonelier than I might have been. If my situation had been different, I'd have turned to my parents for comfort and love. But lacking that option I was going to have to dig deep within my own resources if I was going to survive, never mind prosper.

Finnegan's had in the meantime closed down, so I got a job as manageress at the Suede Centre in Bold Street. But I wasn't happy working there. The shop was too small, although in other circumstances I could have coped with that. In truth, my unhappiness followed me to work like a black cloud. I didn't suffer a nervous breakdown but I was undeniably in a state of near collapse after everything I'd suffered, physically and emotionally, at Ken's hands. Then Fate dealt me a rare good card. Just a matter of weeks earlier I'd met a man – another policeman, heaven help me. His name was Peter Woodburn.

14

A Decent Man

On 25 April 1975 – a little over two months before I finally got Ken out of our flat and out of my life – I was at home alone, drinking in the bath late at night. The phone rang. It was the police. Finnegan's had been broken into. As the manageress, I was one of the two keyholders. Would I please get down to the shop as soon as possible? I knew I wasn't in a fit state to go talking to the police so I asked if they would ring my assistant manageress, Mrs Radcliffe, who was the other keyholder.

Within half an hour, though, my conscience had got the better of me. Radi had been so good to me. She was a woman of sixty-four. Was it really fair to ask her to turn out at that time of night when I was the one who should shoulder the responsibility? So I did my best to sober up, ordered a taxi and waited for it to arrive. Just as I was about to leave, the phone rang again.

'Hello,' said a voice, 'it's Radi.'

I immediately started apologising. 'I'm awfully sorry,' I said. 'I shouldn't have left this to you. I feel terrible about it. I'm coming down there right now.'

She told me she was fine, and then I heard what I thought was a chuckle from her end of the phone. 'I'll tell you something,' she said, 'and you may not want to hear this right now. But I've got a very nice policeman here.'

What on earth was she on about? I told her, 'Radi, I've had policemen up to here.'

She wasn't having any of it, though. 'Believe me,' she persisted, 'he's lovely!'

Be that as it may, my taxi had arrived. I popped a bottle of Drambuie and some whisky into my basket and headed off to the city centre. When I reached Finnegan's, I could see that the burglars had smashed in the shop door; I later found out they'd snatched a handful of men's trousers. It was obvious this was going to be a long night because we'd have to wait while someone boarded up the broken glass and then we'd have to give a statement.

I had spotted Peter as soon as I walked through the door. He was in his motorbike leathers, standing inside the shop. Just before I'd arrived, an old man had turned up to erect some temporary boarding. It wasn't until many years later that Pete told me what the old man had whispered under his breath as I walked into the shop in my trouser suit and four-inch-high platform soles. 'Bloody hell,' he'd said, 'she'd break your back. But you'd die happy.'

Radi was sitting behind the counter. I opened my basket and offered her a drink.

Pete saw the bottle of Drambuie. 'Do you always carry alcohol with you?' he asked. I don't think he was judging me. I think he was genuinely interested.

'Always,' I said. 'Because of the pig I'm married to, I need it to keep me sane.' Then I asked if he'd like a drop.

He said he couldn't, not on duty. 'But I wouldn't mind one later,' he added. When Pete moved out of earshot, Radi looked at me. 'I knew I was right,' she said. 'That police officer likes you.'

About an hour later, the old man had finished boarding up the front of the shop. Pete said that, if Radi and I waited, he'd return his motorbike to the garage and then come back in his police car to the station where we'd be making a statement and give us both a lift home. Radi said that Pete would have to drop me off first as she lived further out. I thought there wasn't any harm in the offer and accepted.

When Pete reappeared he'd changed out of his leathers into his normal uniform, complete with peaked cap. 'Right, ladies,' he said, 'are you ready?' So we got in the car, but before long it became obvious he was going on a detour to drop Radi first.

She dug me in the ribs in the back of the car. 'Told you,' she mouthed.

By the time we reached Gateacre I'd decided I'd invite him in for a coffee if Ken wasn't at home, which was a pretty safe bet since he was hardly ever there. Once inside, we started talking. I told him I was miserable and I'd filed for divorce. But, I explained, the situation was difficult as we were still sleeping under the same roof. 'As a matter of fact,' I went on, 'my husband is one of you lot.'

Pete said nothing.

I asked him if he was married.

Yes, he was, and he produced photographs of his wife from his wallet. He kept telling me how happy he was.

But something wasn't right. 'No, you're not,' I said, 'otherwise you wouldn't keep saying everything's wonderful. Who are you trying to convince?' I told him he didn't seem in the least bit happy.

His expression immediately changed. 'You're right,' he said. 'I'm not happy at all.' It turned out that his wife, Carmen, worked in the furniture trade. She'd been unfaithful to him once before, and now she'd met a chap in London where she went once a year to work for six weeks, and they were having an affair. Pete told me how much he loved her but that it was hopeless.

The following morning I was in the shop when, about eleven o'clock, Pete walked in wearing tight jeans and a yellow voile shirt. I've still got that shirt to this day. He was in town, he said, shopping with his wife and he just wanted to check everything was all right after the robbery. We chatted for a bit and then he was gone. But not for long. On Monday he appeared again. He and another bobby were about to take two prisoners to Manchester in a police van. We had a cup of tea together and another chat.

On Tuesday, he rang me at the shop. Could he take me out the next day? Apparently he'd been egged on by some of his colleagues, although he later told me it took him all his courage to pick up that phone. Wednesday was my day off so I agreed to meet him in the Hanover pub. I know Pete was attracted to me – he told me so later – but I think he felt protective, too. When I walked in the pub that Wednesday lunchtime, I could see he was shocked by my appearance. I may have been smartly dressed, but I was also sporting a black eye and a line of bruises across the bridge of my nose.

The previous evening, when Ken had finally got home, I'd told him I'd met a very nice man, a policeman. 'But not a pig like you,' I said. Ken hadn't taken too kindly to that and had punched me in the face.

I'd been a fool. Why had I provoked him when I knew how he was capable of reacting? It reminded me of my relationship with my mother. On the one hand I'd try and keep out of her way because I hated the beatings. But sometimes a little devil would get the better of me and I'd blurt out something that was bound to provoke violence.

At that stage, Pete still didn't know my husband's name. We were seeing each other regularly and then, about three weeks after the burglary, he and I were having a drink one day when he turned to me and said, 'By the way, I've been meaning to ask you, what your husband's name is?'

So I told him.

His mouth fell open. 'You're married to *him*?' he exclaimed. I don't think he could believe it. 'God almighty, I wouldn't have come within ten miles of your place if I'd known. He's a wicked bastard and violent, too. He thinks with his fists.' Apparently Ken had a terrible reputation as a bully and a bragger who thought nothing of sleeping with other policemen's wives.

On one occasion Pete was coming round to the

flat to have a coffee, and I was sure Ken would be at work so I wasn't worried. But on that particular day Ken lay in bed and didn't get up for work. At about half past ten, as expected, the buzzer went, so I ran to the intercom and whispered to Pete that Ken hadn't gone to work and he should therefore get out of the area sharpish. But it was a small flat and Ken could obviously hear what was going on. He was out of his bedroom at top speed, pulling on a pair of slacks and running down the stairs to the street. However Pete was away before Ken could reach him – although I didn't know that at the time. As Ken came back into the flat he boasted. 'I've put him straight about you.' He hadn't, of course.

I looked at him. 'Ken,' I said, 'why do you care?' He just slammed the bedroom door in my face.

In the weeks that followed, my friendship with Pete deepened and we became lovers; I enjoyed the physical affection after so many loveless months with Ken. Pete and I were each a shoulder for the other to cry on. Our situations were so similar: both of us had partners we still had feelings for, but they were cheating on us and didn't care if we knew. It was good to have Pete to talk to and I know he felt the same about me. He'd listen to my problems. He'd comfort me when Ken hit me. He'd tell me he thought I looked beautiful. We've been together now for over thirty years, married for twenty-seven, and there's not a day passes without him turning to me and saying: 'You know, Kim, truthfully, you haven't aged a month since I first saw you.' What's more, he believes it. It's not true, of course, but it's lovely of him to say so. He's so proud of me – the sweetest, kindest, most gentle man you could ever wish to meet.

By this time I had moved to an airy new studio flat, though in the same area. I'd left the job at the Suede Shop and I was on benefit – just £10 a week, with no possibility of saving – but my new surroundings were really nice and, luckily, Pete was contributing to the rent. There was one big room with a fitted bathroom and kitchen off it, and a hallway leading to my own front door. I stayed there for two years. Pete's house was on the market and, like me, he was filing for divorce – in his case on the grounds of his wife's adultery. When his place sold, he got half the money and moved in with me. Friendship had matured into love. My divorce came through in November 1975; Pete's the following summer.

Both of us had taken our divorces to heart. For all that we'd each been badly treated by our ex-partners, love can take a long time to die. Pete and I were brought together by mutual attraction, of course, but also through having gone through rather similar experiences; and that's how our friendship had grown and how it had developed into love. But it wasn't all plain sailing. I remember we were sitting in my studio flat in Gateacre one day watching television: it was called *Carmen Jones*, an old musical with Harry Belafonte and Dorothy Dandridge. This was before Ken's house had sold. At the end of the film, he said he needed to check that everything was all right at the house and that he'd see me later.

He seemed a bit subdued, but assured me he felt fine. But after he left the flat he went to a call box and phoned his ex-wife, Carmen. Perhaps the film had triggered memories for him. I knew he'd been in touch with her, because not long after Pete had driven off she called me. She'd found out my number, she said, because she'd paid a private detective to check up on me – heaven knows why, since she was the one who'd cheated on Pete.

'You know this man you're going out with,' she continued. 'I thought you ought to know that he's just called me.' Who knows what her game was? I suppose it was the old thing of not wanting him herself but not wanting anyone else to have him, either. 'He says he wants to get back with me,' she stated. I said, 'Thanks for letting me know,' and put the phone down.

I didn't blame Pete for having phoned her. He was in a state of emotional turmoil, and I knew he was a decent guy. But I was upset. When he rang me the next morning, I told him about the conversation I'd had with his ex-wife. 'Look, Pete,' I went on, 'I've never asked you to pretend otherwise – of course you still have feelings for Carmen. Despite everything, I do for Ken. But we mustn't have secrets from each other.' Then I told him we ought to have a couple of days without seeing each other, to get over what had happened. In the event it was to be a lot longer than that, but the experience made us all the stronger.

There was a girl called Gwen who lived in the opposite flat and worked as a purser for Fred Olsen's shipping line. I got talking to her and said I fancied a break. Might there be any jobs going on the *Blenheim*, the ship she was currently working on? As luck would have it the ship's gift shop needed a manageress, something I could easily do with all my experience. She said she'd put in a word for me, and within the day I had the job. Two days later I would be sailing for Madeira, Lanzarote, Tenerife and Las Palmas and then back to Madeira, a thirteen-day round trip. When I told Pete, he was crestfallen. 'You can't go away to sea,' he protested. But I told him I had to – that it was important to put some space between us while I sorted out how I felt about our relationship. My mind was made up.

I then got a call from Pete's mother, Edna, in a further attempt to make me change my mind. She told me her son was broken-hearted because of my decision. I told her I thought he was great and that I'd miss him terribly, but I couldn't deal with what had happened and surely she must understand that. Both Pete and I had been through painful divorces and we were still working through the feelings we'd had for our former partners. I likened it to an extended grieving period.

To me, though, this decision to put physical distance between Pete and myself was achieving more than giving us some mental space to sort out our feelings. I realise now that it was a watershed, a turning point. It was so lovely to have him in my life and he felt the same about me. I'd married my first husband relatively late – I was twenty-nine – and I'd never for a moment dreamt it would end in divorce. I'd been so badly hurt on all fronts: emotionally, physically, financially. I knew Pete wanted to marry me; he'd asked me often enough. But I wasn't ready, and I had to be absolutely sure. I couldn't have dealt with a second failure. And I had a niggling worry at the back of my mind. Were Pete and I clinging to each other because we'd been through such similar circumstances?

I couldn't answer that if I remained too close to the situation; I had to get away. We had been together for eighteen months by this stage, and we had grown very fond of each other – but neither of us could afford another mistake. And I didn't want to hang around with Pete and start arguing with him if he was still going to be tempted to ring Carmen when he was at a low ebb. A clean break was what was needed. Also, I thought it would be a good test of Pete. If he wanted me in my absence, he'd be there for me whenever I came home. And if he didn't, I'd have avoided the mess of another failed relationship.

I never once wavered over my decision, although as the ship sailed out I had a moment of doubt: what on earth was I doing? But I recovered very quickly. This isn't meant to sound harsh, but I felt Pete needed to be taught a lesson, to be given the ultimate test. I thought to myself that, if he loved me enough, he'd chase me. And he did. He rang me. He sent me telegrams. On subsequent sailings he'd meet the ship when it docked in London for the two-day turnaround. He'd be there on the platform at Liverpool Lime Street when I came home on leave.

In the end I worked for Fred Olsen for a year, and I got used to life on board. When I was at sea, I didn't have a worry in the world. I'd been through too much over the last seven or eight years of my life, never mind my childhood. The only good thing that had come out of all these terrible events was that now, in my mid-thirties, I'd developed a new kind of strength. I'd never have walked away from Pete ten years earlier; I'd have clung to him. But now I was no longer a stupid little girl, no longer a victim.

The *Blenheim* was 16,000 tons, quite small for a cruise ship, and carried around four hundred passengers. The gift shop sold perfumes, cosmetics, hosiery, silk scarves – all top-of-the-range stuff – I had two assistants under me. It was quite a boring existence, although I had officer status which meant I could go anywhere I wanted on the ship. In the evening I'd go to the dance hall, a good excuse to put on a pretty dress. And I got a good wage with very little to spend it on except when we docked somewhere and I went ashore. But of course I wasn't doing the job for the money.

After a year, I'd made my decision. My time on the *Blenheim* had served its purpose. Towards the end of 1977 I rang Pete at my flat, where he'd carried on living while I'd been at sea. He asked me where I was.

'I'm about to board a train to Liverpool from London,' I said. 'I've handed in my notice. I'm coming home.'

He was overjoyed. 'Oh, thank God for that!' he responded.

'Well, I think it's about time,' I said, 'that you and I became a permanent fixture.'

I could hear him chuckling down the phone. 'Oh, I'm all for that,' he said. Then he told me he'd meet me off the train – although, when it came to it, I hardly recognised him. He'd had his hair cropped, having thought he wouldn't be seeing me for another two weeks which would give it time to grow, and he had a large, angry red boil at the end of his nose.

As he came running up to me, I couldn't help blurting out, 'What the hell . . .?'

He just said, 'Don't look at the hair! Don't look at the hooter!'

We fell into each other's arms, laughing and kissing, knowing as we couldn't have known with such certainty a year earlier that we were back together – and for ever.

But we couldn't live on love alone. Pete's job in the police was secure enough and he was earning good money, but I needed to find employment for myself. I'd always worked in retail in one way or another, but I was feeling stronger now and decided my next challenge was going to be something completely different. It was time for a change.

Scanning the papers one day, my eye was caught by an advert for a residential social worker at a remand centre for girls aged between ten and sixteen. The idea of working with children appealed to me, so I applied for an interview with the superintendent, an ex-bobby. I told him I had no experience but explained about my rough childhood, and said I thought that experience would stand me in good stead when it came to handling difficult kids. He seemed to accept that. But then I made the mistake of saying that if I could do anything to help them on their way I'd be only too happy. He was a lovely man, but I could see from the look on his face that I'd misread the situation.

'Can I tell you something, love?' he said. 'Out of every hundred little girls who pass through here, about five per cent go and live with someone who gives them a handful of illegitimate kids and beats them on a regular basis. And they're the ones we call our success stories. Good luck!'

None the less he recommended me for an interview with Social Services in Liverpool, and I got the job. Although it was called 'residential' I only had to sleep over one night a week – the rest of the time I slept in the flat I was now sharing with Pete.

The girls used to fight and kick and bite and scream and beat the staff if they could get away with it, but no one ever touched me. I was quite a disciplinarian but never felt threatened, as I told the superintendent.

'I don't want to burst your bubble, love,' he replied, 'but have you seen the size of you? Would *you* attack you? Because I wouldn't!' The girls were allowed out sometimes at weekends, but invariably they'd be brought back by the police who would find them on street corners saying, 'Business, love?' to any passing man. They'd swear blind they'd only been asking the time, but I'd just laugh at them.

'What? At two o'clock in the morning?' I'd say. 'Get out of here!'

We'd end up laughing together. The superintendent had been right – they were never going to make anything of their lives. But I couldn't help liking their spirit.

A year later, when Pete and I bought a small, three bedroom semi-detached house in Formby, I asked for a transfer to a nearer remand centre, St Christopher's in Crosby; my journey into Liverpool would have been too difficult from there. With my professional life now sorted out – I stayed at St Christopher's for six years in the end – I was ready to make the ultimate personal commitment.

Pete and I finally married on 2 August 1979 at a registry office in Southport. His mum and dad were there, as were my Uncle Neville, his wife, Pat, and their two sons, Ian and Graham. I wore a black suit and suede shoes, my hair piled high. Pete was in a beautiful pinstriped suit. And, unlike the way I'd felt on the day I married Ken, I didn't have even a shadow of a doubt about marrying Pete; I knew we'd be for ever. Afterwards, we went back to his parents' house for drinks and the beautiful cake his father, George, a retired master baker, had made for us. It was a very happy occasion, but then this was a marriage founded on common decency. Pete and I are completely relaxed in each other's company. We have a laugh together but we're not afraid to cry in front of each other either. We're soulmates.

In 1982, I got it into my head to take Pete to Portsmouth to introduce him to my mother. I was forty; she was fifty-nine. We hadn't set eyes on each other since I'd told her to get out of my father's house just before my sixteenth birthday. I hadn't spoken to her since she phoned me out of the blue at drama school at the end of the sixties. That might have been the end of that. But something still gnawed away at my mind. It would have been easy to say that I no longer cared about what she'd done to me or what she might think of me today; but it wouldn't have been true. I needed to know two things: why had she given me, of all her children, such a wretched childhood, and was there anything in her that now made her regret the way she'd behaved?

A lot of water had flowed under the bridge. Perhaps time had mellowed her. Perhaps she was now more passive, more prepared to talk in a calm way and lay to rest some of the ghosts that had haunted me all my life. I'd be lying if I didn't also admit that I knew I had a good marriage to Pete, a relationship that was going to last. Part of me wanted to show him off to my mother. The only policemen who had ever crossed her path had been summoned by neighbours because of her drunken behaviour. Now here I was, married to one. I was proud of Pete. Would my mother be proud for me, too?

I got her phone number from Uncle Nev and rang her to say I'd like to come and see her. I'd describe her reaction as indifferent. She wasn't full of the joys of spring at the prospect of my visit, but she didn't discourage me either. I wonder now if she thought she might touch me for some money, but if so, she didn't say anything to that effect on the phone.

I simply didn't know what to expect when I arrived. My single hope was that she would unlock the mysteries that had tortured me for so many years. But if it turned out to be a painful experience, I had a safety net in Pete. Afterwards, whatever she might have said and done in the past and during this visit, I would have the security of a loving relationship with a good man. I wouldn't be returning to an empty life with no one to support me.

When she opened the front door to her house in Westfield Road I had cause for hope. She didn't look too bad. Her hair was dyed a dark brown, she was wearing full make-up and her nails were as immaculate as ever. She'd lost weight since the last time I'd seen her, but then she was nearly sixty. She was wearing a brown printed dress. She greeted us – no peck on the cheek, though, no hug – and we followed her inside.

She went into the kitchen to make a pot of tea as my two youngest half-sisters, Caroline and Janet, introduced themselves to me. They were in their early twenties by then, but they'd been born after I'd left home so we were strangers to each other. I can't say they were unpleasant to me, but they were distinctly cool. Then Richard appeared; I think he had a job working on the lifeboats, although this was his day off. My mother came back from the kitchen with the tea and the others left the room, leaving just Pete and me to talk to her.

I needed the answer to the one question above all others that had troubled me for as far back as I could remember and there was no point in delaying asking it. I took a deep breath.

'There's something I want to ask you,' I said. 'Why did you hate me so much?'

My mother didn't even hesitate. 'Because you're too like your fucking father,' she replied, cool as a cucumber. 'I always hated you.'

It was as if all the intervening years had simply rolled away. She'd spoken to me in exactly the same way as she'd done thirty years earlier. Time hadn't softened her in any way whatsoever. To this day, I don't think Pete can quite comprehend that a mother, any mother, could say and feel that about her own child.

'Anyway,' she continued, changing the subject, 'why are you wearing glasses?'

I told her it was because I'd been born virtually blind in my right eye.

She couldn't have been less interested. 'Oh, really?' she said. 'First I've heard of it.'

I asked after Mac. Apparently he'd been dead a year. My mother told me a photograph of her was found in his wallet, and claimed to be surprised. 'Don't ask me why,' she said.

I looked at her. 'Because he loved you,' I explained. She just shrugged her shoulders. I asked her if she missed him.

'I miss his fifty pounds a week,' she said. Mac had gone on giving her money even after their youngest, Janet, was sixteen.

I said, 'Mother, that's a wicked thing to say.' But she didn't care.

She didn't seem curious to know how my life had gone since we'd last seen each other. I'd brought a video of my appearance on *Pebble Mill at One* talking about knitting designs – I was quite proud of that – and I asked if she'd like to see it. 'Oh, if you like,' she said. So Pete put it into the machine, but she could barely be bothered to watch the screen. Nor did she ask Pete anything about himself or how we'd met. She spoke only when she was spoken to – and this was a woman who'd talk nineteen to the dozen if she was in the mood. I'd taken her a bottle of Tia Maria because I knew that was one of her favourite drinks, but she didn't open it while we were there. The longer I sat there, the more obvious it was that she felt nothing at all for me. She gave every indication that she was simply bored by our presence. So I asked her if she fancied going out to look at the shops. I thought it might create a new mood.

'Not really,' she said, 'I hate window-shopping. I'd rather buy something or not bother.'

But we needed to get out of the house, so I more or less forced her to come in the car with Pete and me. We stopped at the stores in Commercial Road and she was totally uninterested.

'I can't afford anything,' she said, 'so I'd sooner be at home.' I suppose she hoped I'd dip into my purse, but I didn't have money to spare.

After the unsuccessful shopping trip we went back to Westfield Road and Pete and I suggested we could take my mother, Richard, Caroline and Janet out to a local restaurant for a meal. Nothing fancy, but our treat. We went in two cars – Pete's and Richard's – but I don't know why we made the effort. There was no warmth, no easy flow of conversation. When it came to paying the bill, Pete got out his cheque book. My mother's eyes were out on stalks and she watched him intently as he wrote his bank card number on the back. Perhaps she hoped he'd write one out for her.

We left the restaurant and went back to the house after for ten minutes. We'd arrived in Portsmouth around two and it was now about 10.30. Pete and I had had enough. There were no thank yous, no kisses goodbye, nothing. I wouldn't let her see what I was feeling, but I just couldn't believe that a woman who had treated her daughter so badly hadn't learnt any sort of lesson by the eve of her sixtieth birthday. She hadn't, though. She'd been no different that day from how she'd been throughout my entire miserable childhood.

As we drove away from Portsmouth I felt angry and sad, but my overwhelming emotion was one of disappointment. Looking back, I realised that I'd never really believed my mother would have matured into a reasonable middle-aged woman.

But I'd hoped for a suggestion of remorse, a hint of apology. Yet it was perfectly plain that she hadn't missed me for a moment. She couldn't have cared less whether I was alive or dead. Still, I consoled myself with the thought that I might have failed but that at least I'd tried.

In a strange way it was a liberating experience. It had been a waste of time and effort, but now I was free to let go. And so it proved. That meeting was the last time I saw my mother until I looked into her coffin in April 2000.

15

Loose Ends

You don't have the sort of upbringing I had and shrug it off lightly. Between February 1958 and her death in April 2000 I only spoken to my mother once on the phone and saw her once in person. And I didn't see my father for years and years after I moved out of his rented cottage in Upton, across the water from Liverpool. Nevertheless both of them continued to lurk in the shadows of my life.

I remember on one occasion, when I was working as a demonstrator for Carmen rollers, I was sent to a store in Portsmouth. I had no wish to turn up on my mother's doorstep, but I couldn't help being curious to discover whether she was still alive and up to her usual tricks. After work one day I decided to pay a visit to the police station in Cosham, where she'd been better known by the local constabulary than any of them would have wished. I asked for a particular bobby who was the one most frequently despatched to Mablethorpe Road after my mother's drunken screaming matches with Mac.

Eventually, he appeared from the back office. 'Good heavens,' he said, 'I know you, don't I?'

I smiled. 'That's right. I'm Pat McKenzie.'

'Well, you've certainly blossomed,' he said.

I told him I'd left the area years ago, to get away from my mother.

'And you did the right thing,' said the bobby. 'She's still around and yes, she's still fighting fit, still rioting all over Wymering.'

No surprises there, then.

It was while I was in Portsmouth on that occasion that I saw my half-brother Neil, again. Seventeen by then, and training to be a hairdresser, he loved the work but was having a bad time with my mother. He towered over her, but that didn't stop her giving him a tongue-lashing if she was in the mood. When it all got too much for him he'd go and stay the night somewhere – with a mate, I imagine – to keep out of her way.

My Uncle Neville had told Neil I was in town, so he turned up at the large bed and breakfast where I was staying. He told me that our mother was drinking all the time and always looking for trouble. If he'd stayed away from home for the night she'd turn up at the hairdresser's and start banging on the window. It obviously caused him acute embarrassment. He hated all the upset and he was worried, too, that she might lose him his job – something that she did indeed achieve in the end – just as she'd done with Mac at the Flexible Packaging Company.

I'd been fond of Neil when he was little and I wanted to help him now if I could, so I suggested he came and lived with me in Liverpool. I told him he'd enjoy life there. There were lots of nice salons and a good rock 'n' roll scene. If he went home and packed a bag without our mother seeing, I told him, I'd book him into a room in the B&B the following night and we'd head up north the day afterwards when I'd finished my demonstrating stint. He seemed really relieved and said he'd see me next day after work.

Sure enough, he turned up with his little bag – he looked such a forlorn sight – and we started chatting about his future. But just as I was explaining about life in Liverpool, the landlady knocked on my door and said my mother was in Reception. Heaven knows how she'd found out where I was, but I can only assume Neil must have said something to her. She didn't want to see me, though; she wanted to know if Neil was with me.

As soon as he knew our mother was downstairs, he panicked. 'I've got to go, got to go,' he cried.

I tried to calm him down, told him he could stay with me, that we'd be off to Liverpool in the morning. But he wouldn't listen. He picked up his bag and fled. He was frightened silly of that woman. The next time I saw him was at our mother's funeral.

To a certain extent I'd kept tabs on my mother down the years via her younger brother, my Uncle Neville, who'd lived in Portsmouth all his life and got all the bits and bobs of family gossip. He once told me that he went to see my mother and my name came up, but what she'd said about me was so unbelievable that he could never bring himself to repeat it.

'Pat,' he'd said to her, 'this is your daughter you're talking about. How on earth could you say such a thing?'

She couldn't have cared less, apparently. More recently, I asked him to tell me exactly what it was my mother had said about me. He claimed he couldn't remember, but I know that wasn't true. He was trying to protect my feelings.

Nev's relationship with my mother had never been easy. He remembers a time from way back in 1947 when his mother (my Grandma Mary) had fallen ill – so ill, in fact, that it was feared she might die. Nev's older brother Gordon was in the Merchant Navy at the time, and he was worried about where Nev would live if Grandma didn't survive. Back home on leave, Gordon explained to Nev that because of the nature of his job he couldn't look after him himself, but he gave him a choice: he could live with my mother, or with his father, or he could go into a home. Years later Nev bumped into my mother and Mac having a drink together in a pub. So he joined them. She started boasting to Mac about how well she and Nev got on, how close they'd always been. Nev wasn't having any of it, and that's when he told her about the options Gordon had presented him with if Grandma had died at the end of the forties. He looked my mother straight in the eye. 'I told him, Pat,' said Nev, 'that I'd sooner live in a home than with you or my father. That's how close you and I were.' He was furious with her for distorting the truth. In fact, he didn't speak to her again for the rest of her life.

Only recently Nev told me that, towards the end of his fifties, Mac at last met a nice woman. I was so glad to hear that; it was the least he deserved after putting up with my mother for so long. That must have been ten years or more after he'd left my mother for the last time. But, sadly, he was to die relatively young. He was playing darts in his local pub and he'd lost. The rule was that the loser had to buy the drinks. Mac had just paid for a round when he dropped dead at the bar from a massive heart attack. He was only sixty-three.

When she died, almost twenty years later, my mother was buried next to him in the local cemetery. And yet my sister Gezzie has always claimed our mother didn't want to lie in the ground next to Mac. But it does seem odd to me that there was still a vacant plot beside his nineteen years after he'd been laid to rest. It's one of the many unsolved mysteries of my huge and strange family. But maybe my half-brothers and -sisters arranged it. Who knows? Either way, it's my considered opinion she should think herself privileged to lie beside a man like Mac.

Then there was my father, by the 1990s a shadowy figure whom I hadn't seen or heard from in almost forty years. In 1995 Pete and I had returned from America, where we'd been living. I'd always wanted to see the States for myself and had persuaded Pete to come with me and to try our luck as housekeeper and houseman. It turned out to be quite an adventure! When we got back we went to stay with his mum, Edna, in Liverpool while we searched for work. We didn't want to be there, but we had no money and so no choice. We decided to get taken on by a brewery to train as pub managers, which would get us away from Liverpool and put a roof over our heads. But it didn't work out: the hours were long and our living conditions were disgusting. So we returned to live with Pete's mother and signed on with an employment agency which specialised in housekeepers and housemen. In June 1997, a couple of months before we landed a wonderful position in a fashionable part of London, the phone rang one day.

Pete answered it. I heard him say into the receiver, 'Who? Her father? Are you sure?' He looked at me.

'Don't be daft,' I said. 'He must be dead by now.'

Pete shook his head. 'Does he have a Scottish accent?'

I nodded and he passed me the phone. 'I thought you were dead,' I said.

'No,' said my father. 'Betty and I went to live in Pembrokeshire.' They'd had two more children after Jean: another daughter, Barbara, and at last a longed for boy, Ronnie.

'Oh, so you got your son in the end,' I said, remembering my childhood as an unwanted second daughter. But he didn't rise to my sarcasm.

I asked my father how he'd traced me.

He'd gone to Portsmouth, he said, and knocked on my mother's door. Betty wouldn't go with him; she wanted nothing to do with it. My mother had invited him in but she refused to tell him where

Gezzie lived and she had no idea of my whereabouts. 'They won't want to see you,' she'd told him.

But while he was sitting in her lounge Richard picked up the local newspaper and started reading it. My parents were talking when Richard suddenly interrupted. 'Good God,' he said, 'Graeme's in the paper for a traffic offence!' Graeme was one of Gloria's two sons. When my father left, he got a copy of that paper and scoured it until he came to the item about the traffic offence, which gave Graeme's name and address. My father got a taxi there and it turned out to be Gloria's high-rise flat; Graeme was back living with her at the time.

Gloria wasn't unpleasant to him, but after all this time she wasn't really interested in having anything to do with our father. But he did manage to get out of her that my married name was Woodburn and that I lived somewhere in the Liverpool area. Gezzie had phoned me occasionally when I was living in America so she had a rough idea of my movements; she'd obviously passed on that information to our father. There were only ten Woodburns in the telephone book and he'd rung each one in turn until he found me.

Then I asked him what had prompted him to get in touch, and he mumbled something about wanting to find out how I was getting on. A friend whom I later told about this telephone conversation said she didn't think my father had been in touch for any other reason than that he was getting old and wanted to be at peace. In other words, he wasn't doing it for me – or indeed for Gloria – but for himself.

Whatever the explanation, it felt very strange talking to him after all this time. He said he'd like to meet me, but I was nervous. It seemed a bit late to forge any kind of relationship, since we'd never had one in the first place. When I told him that my childhood memories were so unhappy he immediately blamed my mother for my rotten upbringing.

'Yes,' I said, 'but you were my dad.'

He protested. 'I was in the Marines for twenty-two years.'

Perfectly true but, as I pointed out, he never once sent me a birthday card.

'I know,' he agreed, 'but I didn't know when your birthday was.'

That upset me so much. He couldn't seem to see that that single remark told the whole story. In the end, though, I relented. I said that Pete and I would come and see him and Betty in Wales on Fathers' Day, the following week. Deep down, I needed to know what he really felt about me. I needed to find out what this man was all about, to try to solve the mystery of my childhood. My mother hadn't acknowledged me. I had to believe my father would. I had to believe I was somebody's child. I still had a deep-rooted need to belong.

So Pete and I drove to Haverfordwest in Pembrokeshire to visit my father and Betty in their run-down council bungalow. I took a bottle of whisky for him and a box of Cadbury's Milk Tray for her. To be honest, I was quite intrigued to see what the old so-and-so looked like. I was certainly surprised when he opened the front door. I recognised him straightaway, and he looked marvellous – he could have passed for a man twenty years younger. He was seventy-nine by then, and had scarcely changed from when I'd seen him last in 1961.

My father seemed pleased to see me. He kissed me and gave me a hug. Betty cooked us a nice meal. Neither of them was especially interested in what had happened in my life since they'd last seen me, but they were friendly enough – much more so than my mother had been when I'd taken Pete to meet her. Jean, apparently, had been a bit of a naughty girl. She had six kids and some of them had been a bit wild. Dad and Betty didn't have much to do with her, they said, although she didn't live far away. Ronnie lived with his girlfriend in Bath. But it was Barbara, just on the point of marrying her boyfriend, who was clearly the favourite.

There were photographs of her on the wall on her graduation day and she popped up in conversation all the time. In fact, he called her while we were there.

'Hello, Boo Boo,' he said to her down the telephone. 'It's Dad here.'

That cut right through me. I'd never known anything like that sort of affection from him in my whole life.

On 14 August 1997 Pete and I took up our new job in London. In the weeks that followed, I'd ring my father – he'd ask me to call him on the night Betty went to bingo – or he'd ring me. But we didn't see each other – I was too busy. A couple of months went by when I didn't make any contact. Eventually, my father called me: he wanted to know whether Pete was stopping me from phoning him.

I told him, 'No, Dad, of course not. But, honestly, what's the point? Anyway, Betty obviously isn't keen on the two of us talking. I don't want to have to ring when she's out. I'm too old for all of this.'

We didn't speak for the next three years until we were in touch about my mother's death.

By that time, our jobs in London were coming to an end and Pete and I had managed to put enough money together to enable us to buy a small house on a private estate in Pembrokeshire. When we'd been to see my father and Betty in the summer of 1997, we'd fallen in love with that part of the world. Our savings wouldn't have bought us anything in London, so we thought we'd look in that area while we lived off our state benefit and looked for another job as we headed towards our retirement. Before we moved into our house, we rented a flat in nearby Littlehaven from Barbara and her husband; they charged us £300 a month, which was very reasonable.

But that move to be on my father's doorstep wasn't entirely motivated by financial considerations. I'd given up on my mother completely. I'd been to see her and she'd made it quite clear that time hadn't mellowed her in any way, shape or form. To be fair, I also knew in my heart that my father didn't really love me. He'd allowed forty years of his life to slip by before contacting me again. In the end, though, he was my dad and hope springs eternal. Perhaps in whatever years that were left to him we'd build a sort of belated love. I began seeing him quite often. I think he was pleased to have the company and he'd tell me that he loved me, but I didn't really believe him – his words rang false in my ears. He hadn't known me properly in my childhood. He hadn't seen me for almost all my adulthood. It seemed too late in the day to accept that he'd suddenly started loving me now. And yet I had this almost foolish need to believe that it just might be possible.

After the shock of the way I'd been treated at my mother's funeral, I never gave up hope that at least my remaining parent might somehow show me he was glad that I was his daughter. And I will say this: my father and I were very alike in some ways. Pete had noticed it immediately when he met my father for the first time. We had the same blue eyes, the same sense of humour. We seemed to get along fine and I felt that he and I were becoming quite close, even if I knew it could only now be on a superficial basis. But it gave me a fleeting glimpse of what my life might have been like if I'd had a decent mum and dad. It may have been second best but it was better than nothing – and I wasn't getting any younger. I still desperately wanted to belong.

I decided I wanted to pay for him and Betty to go and stay in a nice hotel for a week's holiday, and he said afterwards that he hadn't had such a good time in all his life. A few weeks later we went with my father, Betty and Barbara to meet Ronnie and his girlfriend in Bath. It was around this time that Dad who was such a fit man, still perfectly capable of mowing his own lawn – started complaining of a bad pain in his left shoulder. The doctor eventually diagnosed it as a virus in the muscle.

But it didn't get any better, so he was sent for an X-ray. When the results came back, they revealed a tumour on his lungs.

Barbara was the one who rang me with the news. She never called me in normal circumstances, so I could tell she was worried. But after that she and Betty were the two who talked in private to the doctor and I began to feel excluded, so I stayed away from the hospital for a week. My father seemed to be siding with Betty and Barbara, and yet had told me he wanted me back in his life. I'd come to live near him. I'd never breathed a word about the way he'd behaved to me all those years before when we were alone together in the pub. And then Jean called. Because of my father's illness, she'd been seeing more of her parents. She wanted to know why I hadn't been to the hospital for the last week and I explained that I found the situation rather awkward.

'Never mind that,' she said. 'He wants to see you.'

So a couple of days later Pete and I went to the hospital. I didn't know it then, but it was to be the last time I ever saw my father. That month – it was February 2001 – Pete and I were due to take up a job as housekeeper and houseman with a nice family in Norway. I was terribly undecided about going, with my father being ill. But I gave him my address and he even wrote to me while I was there – not that he remembered my birthday, though, at the end of March. I stood by the post-box at the end of the drive at the house in Oslo, willing the postman to bring me a birthday card from my father. But nothing ever arrived.

In July we came home for a holiday and I went to see my doctor for some pills. I asked him how Dad was doing.

He looked surprised. 'I'm sorry to have to tell you, but your father died two weeks ago. Didn't you know?'

Betty hadn't told me, so I didn't get the opportunity of attending his funeral. To this day I don't know whether he was buried or cremated, and I've never heard anything from Betty. I don't even know the date of his death. It was all so sad. The previous year, I'd been cut to the core by my treatment at my mother's funeral. And now my father had died and I hadn't even been there to say my goodbyes.

The last piece of the jigsaw fell into place that summer when the details of my mother's estate were revealed. It was discovered after her death that she had £20,000 to her name. Gloria told me about it. I asked her where she thought our mother had got the money, and she said it must have been from her own father, Grandma Mary's husband, Robert. My mother was always his favourite and most like him in temperament. Gloria then explained that our seven half-brothers and -sisters wanted to divide the money between them. We both thought that was wrong; we were her children, too. The money, such as it was, ought to be split nine ways. There was no will, and in such cases the law of the land decrees that all the children should be equal beneficiaries.

I wrote a letter to ask about the distribution of the money but I never got a reply; and I never got a penny. I honestly didn't care: my attitude was to let them get on with it. I'd never had anything all my life, so why start now? As to whether my mother had left any instructions that I should be denied what little I was entitled to, I simply don't know. Not that it mattered any more because, just three years later, my life was to take its most extraordinary twist yet.

16

How Clean Is Your House?

I turned sixty in March 2002. Pete is three years younger than me. My plan had been to wait until he was sixty when he'd qualify for his police pension, and then we'd retire. We already owned our small, detached house in Wales. What with my state pension, Pete's police pension and no mortgage, we'd get by. For the past eighteen years – eleven of them in America, the remaining seven in the UK and Norway – we'd been working as housekeeper and houseman in some fabulous houses for a wide variety of employers, some fabulous, some not. After so many years of scrimping and saving and half-breaking my back looking after all these houses, I felt I'd earned my retirement.

Mine had been a life of stark contrasts: from the lows of a wretched childhood at the hands of my brutal mother, through the unforgettable sadness of losing my baby son and the misery of my failed first marriage, to the wonderful high of the enduring happiness I'd found with my second husband. Now I was determined that Pete and I should spend our final years of employment in a perfect job. And we found it – or, rather, the agency on whose books we were found it for us. We'd come back from Norway for good in July and were back at home in Wales when we got a call. There was a Saudi Arabian sheik who owned a house in Kent that he only visited once a year for six weeks with his family, and he was the most civilised employer you could imagine. We started working for him in mid-July 2002. He arrived on 1 August with his family and entourage, and was gone by the first week in September. The rest of the time was our own, as long as we kept the house and garden in pristine condition. We had our own apartment in the grounds, with a view of the Kent countryside and lots of sheep. We'd found peace at last.

The phone call I took in January 2003 was from Jane Urquhart, boss of Greycoat Placements, the London domestic agency that had been the source of many of our jobs. She's a nice woman, very friendly, very posh, with what I call a far-back voice – straight out of Agatha Christie. She'd been contacted by a production company who were looking for someone with housekeeping experience to take part in a possible TV project. Would I be interested?

'Don't be so daft.' I said. 'I'm sixty. Who'd take on an old broad like me?'

But she wouldn't budge, and in the end I reluctantly agreed that she could give them my phone number.

Within twenty minutes, someone called Victoria Coker was on the line. She was an assistant producer, she explained, with a company called Talkback. She didn't go into much detail but we had a chat and at the end she said I'd made her laugh. She wanted to know whether I'd be prepared to come to London for an interview. They'd send a car, she said.

To tell the truth, I wasn't all that excited because I wasn't really sure what, if anything, was on offer, and I never for one moment thought it would lead to anything. On the other hand, I had nothing to lose and so I said yes.

The following week, Pete and I were driven up to the Talkback offices behind Oxford Street. I was led into a room and asked to sit down, and a video camera was placed on the table in front of me. And then Victoria began asking me lots of questions.

'How long have you been cleaning?' she said.

'Too bloody long!' I replied.

She roared with laughter.

I said, 'I've worked for some dirty beggars in my

time.' I wouldn't name any names but for some reason, as I talked, she was in hysterics.

'Oh, you are funny,' she giggled.

'Me?' I said. 'I don't think I'm in the least bit funny. But I'll tell you something. I do like cleaning. Always have.'

This went on for a bit, and then she stopped the camera. She explained that I wouldn't hear from her for two weeks because the tape of my interview had to be circulated to her bosses at Talkback and then to the people at Channel 4 who were commissioning the show. She still didn't tell me exactly what the show was going to be about. But what did I care? I'd had a bit of fun. I never thought I'd see her again. As I was leaving, though, she put her hand on my arm. 'By the way, Kim,' she said, 'we know when we've found the right person.'

We were driven home and I soon put the experience from my mind. Two weeks later – it was now getting towards the end of January – the telephone rang. It was Victoria. Would I come for what she called a proper audition? She said, 'Everyone at Talkback and Channel 4 loved the tape.'

I couldn't believe my ears. 'They must be bloody nuts!' I told her. Still she made no mention of my role in whatever this show was to be, and she didn't give any hints as to its format. Nor did I ask. But evidently there was a friend of one of the girls in the Talkback offices who lived in an untidy flat. They'd send a car for me the following Monday and take me to this girl's place somewhere in west London. 'We want you to scrutinise her surroundings,' said Victoria, 'and tell her what you think of how she lives.' No problem.

Everything went according to plan, and I arrived at the flat at the beginning of the following week. That's when I first saw Aggie MacKenzie. I'd no idea who she was, what she was called or the role she was to play in this audition. But I do remember thinking, 'Who's that funny little woman? She looks like Harry Potter.' Aggie later told me I made her think of Hagrid in drag, which makes us about even.

There to greet Victoria and me were the producer, Stephanie Harris, the cameraman, Jules Seymour, and the girl whose flat it was. Stephanie turned to me and said, 'I'd like you to take the girl round the flat and give her your reaction.'

I said, 'I'm very blunt.'

Stephanie looked pleased. 'We *want* you to be blunt,' she said. She then asked Aggie to accompany me. That made me think she'd be the presenter of the programme and my role would be the cleaner-cum-housekeeper.

Our first port of call was the bathroom. Oh, the state of it! I said, 'How long since you last cleaned your toilet, you dirty little beggar? There's pee all over the seat. You must have men here. They always pebbledash a wide area.' I could hear people chuckling behind my back. Then we moved on to the kitchen. 'Well, this is a flaming comic opera, isn't it?' I said. 'You look so clean yourself, and yet you live like this. Talk about fur coat, no knickers!' Everyone was roaring with laughter. And so we carried on. When we'd been through all the rooms, Stephanie explained that, one way or the other, I wouldn't hear from her until the end of the following week. No matter. I'd enjoyed myself. I know my job when it comes to cleaning, and I'd long ago realised that I enjoy putting on a bit of a performance. But if that was the end of it, so be it.

Three days later, the phone rang. It was Stephanie Harris. She said, 'Kim, we'd like to offer you the job of co-presenter of seven half-hour shows of a new television series to be called *How Clean Is Your House?*'

I said, 'I beg your pardon?' At the time, I was earning £12,000 a year before tax working for the sheik. 'And we're willing to pay you £2,000 a show,' she said. 'Would that be acceptable?'

I nearly fell through the floor. That was £14,000 – more than my annual salary!

Stephanie was still talking. Would it be all right to send someone from wardrobe to discuss my clothes? And there'd need to be a meeting about hair and make-up. Also, she was keen to start filming soon. Was I free from 7 February? We'd be going to a farm near Tunbridge Wells. I couldn't take it all in.

So began a chapter in my life that I'd have dismissed as fanciful if it had been predicted by a fortune-teller. They kitted me out in skimpy skirts and short, boxy jackets, with my hair piled high and plaited on top of my head – I normally wear it tied loose at the back. I think they wanted Aggie and me to look as comical as possible side by side. I didn't mind. They also seemed to want a sort of good cop, bad cop routine, although I'm not sure they realised that at the beginning. Aggie was the more serious, scientific one; I was encouraged to be no-holds-barred, admonishing all these people for the terrible state of their houses.

To be honest, I don't think either of us thought we could work with the other one. We're such total opposites. I see now, though, that that was the intention. In fact, when Stephanie first offered me the job she said we might not be aware of it but Aggie and I were pure chemistry on screen. She seemed to know what she was talking about and she had a lot of experience, so I took what she said on trust.

I know Aggie was a bit nervous at the beginning

but I never was. I knew my subject inside out and I've never taken any notice of the camera – it might as well not be there. We're so different, but we found a way of working together and everyone seemed happy with what we were doing – that's the way it's been ever since. Channel 4 seemed excited, too. After Stephanie had seen the first two episodes, she told us she knew the show was going to be a hit.

'I hope you can both cope with being famous,' she said, 'because that's what's going to happen.'

How right she was! But I don't think even she could have predicted the speed of our success. We'd made five shows of the seven when the first one went out. It was an instant hit. Suddenly you couldn't open a newspaper, it seemed, without seeing Aggie and me staring back at you. And people wrote the funniest things. Someone said that I looked like a cross between Mother Teresa and Madam Whiplash. Someone else said I'd make a wonderful dominatrix. I didn't mind. To tell the truth, it was a great thrill!

We were asked if we'd do two extra shows so that the first series could run for nine weeks. Not long afterwards, Channel 4 and Talkback took us out to lunch and asked if we'd do sixteen shows for the second series. He also had in mind a series called *Too Posh to Wash*, about personal hygiene. We ended up doing six of those. We couldn't believe what was happening. And then the Americans started sitting up and taking notice. They loved the format of the show but they didn't want to find two Americans to present it; they wanted us – and for twenty-two shows! And so it just grew and grew. Our book of cleaning tips was a bestseller. The show has now been sold to over thirty countries around the world.

I can't go outside my front door now without being recognised. I'm not complaining. But then Aggie and I have sorted out an awful lot of filthy houses in full sight of the viewing public, both here and in the States. And television is a very powerful medium. If people stop and talk to me – and I'm happy to say they often do – they almost always ask the same two questions: do we doctor the houses or are they really that bad and which are the worst houses Aggie and I have ever had to clean? And the same two always seem to come to mind.

Bob was a bachelor in his late forties who lived in a terraced house in Northampton. He was keen on amateur dramatics and worked at the local council rubbish tip. And that was the problem. When a long-term relationship ended Bob let himself go, allowing his house to become more and more like the dump where he worked. The trouble was, he started bringing sacks of other people's discarded rubbish home with him, in case they contained something he might find useful. And when he found little to interest him, he just left the rubbish lying on the floor.

You cannot begin to imagine the state of his house. In his own words, he'd become 'a disgusting, disgraceful slob' who showered at work because his own bathroom was so filthy. In fact, when Aggie sent samples gathered from beneath the taps in his sink they were found to contain salmonella. A strain of E. coli was found in his bedroom. In the kitchen, there were mildewed carcasses in the oven where he hadn't cooked a meal for nearly ten years. The air in the sitting room was dangerously contaminated, so it wasn't surprising that Bob had developed asthma. Even the cat had done a runner!

When we called in the council, it took their workmen over six hours to clear more than four tonnes of rubbish from inside the house. Bob had let the situation spiral out of control, and he hadn't known where to start to get back the house that, he told us, used to be his pride and joy. When we allowed him back in again to see the transformation that had taken place he broke down and cried. He promised never to let the situation get out of control again, and when Aggie and I returned a month or so later he'd been true to his word. The place could have done with a bit of dusting, but Bob had been given back his self-confidence. He now had pride in his surroundings once more.

Phyllis was a completely different kettle of fish. A highly intelligent middle-aged American, she had lived for many years in a beautiful Georgian flat in the heart of London's Kensington, next door to actor Terence Stamp. She worked as an art dealer, with a stall in a local market, and her apartment was full of paintings of all shapes and sizes. Unfortunately, it was also full of the accumulation of years of grease and dust and dirt. Touch any surface and it was sticky. The light switches were covered in grime, as were the skirting boards and walls.

Phyllis was an enthusiastic cook but she never cleaned up after herself, never threw anything away. She'd buy fresh herbs but throw them into the fridge on top of old, rotting ones. We found spice jars almost ten years beyond their Sell By dates. When Aggie took a swab from her fridge, the lab found bacteria that could have caused gastro-enteritis and even gangrene. Another swab, from the phone, revealed organisms that normally live in the intestine and that could have triggered urinary tract infections. Phyllis blamed her dog but, as Aggie pointed out, dogs don't make many phone calls!

Our wonderful army of cleaners moved in and scraped and washed and scrubbed and vacuumed the flat until it was restored to sparkling condition. Phyllis was thrilled. And when we returned two weeks later, it really did seem as if she was back on top of her housekeeping again. She even gave us a painting she'd done of the two of us.

But worse than Bob, worse than Phyllis – much, much worse – was a woman chosen for a show that never made it to the screen. Let's call her Jo. She was a woman in her forties, a buxom wench who lived not far from Brighton and owned five horses which she kept stabled down the road. Aggie and I are used to being hit by a wave of bad odours when we enter uncared for houses. But this one was in a league of its own. Quite literally, we were gagging for breath. Even from the middle of the road we could smell something odd. As we walked through the front door, we discovered why.

There were sixteen cats, ten dogs, three sick ducks, rabbits, birds and a lamb wearing a nappy wandering round the house. She rarely took any of them out. The floor was covered in faeces, with bundles of hay and newspapers thrown down to cover the filth. When you tried to walk anywhere you were slipping and sliding, your shoes picking up the muck as you moved around. There wasn't a single surface that wasn't covered in animal or bird droppings of one sort or another, an accumulation of many years of faeces and filth. The fumes they gave off were so pungent that our eyes were streaming.

Jo was an educated woman but I've always maintained that cleaning has no class distinction. You can be a toff living in filth; equally, you can be dirt poor but live in spotless surroundings. Upstairs, we came across a Great Dane, a beautiful dog, sitting next to a mountain of excrement. Every time he felt the call of nature, he'd simply add a bit more to the teetering pile.

But perhaps the most shocking room of all was her bedroom. The bed was covered in animal faeces, the sheets stuck together by the filth. She'd sleep on this bed, the Great Dane and the nappy-clad lamb lying next to her. It was something out of one's worst nightmares. It was while we were in this room that there was a knock at the front door. It was the police. Jo was under arrest for handling fraudulent cheques. We begged the police not to take her away for too long: we had a shooting schedule and we didn't want to get too far behind.

They promised they'd bring her back as quickly as possible and they were as good as their word: she was returned at 2pm. But not long afterwards there was another knock at the door. This time it was the police accompanied by the RSPCA. You could understand why. Those animals were living in conditions that could only be described as cruel. In the end, a decision was made by the top brass at Talkback not to continue filming a woman who was facing criminal charges. We never saw her again. But Aggie and I always say that Jo's story would have been the one that no one would ever have forgotten.

People sometimes ask how I know I'm famous, and I always say the same thing. I knew it when Oprah Winfrey devoted a whole show to Aggie and me. I'll never forget it. It was 2004 and our American TV series was only about a third of the way through its first run. A call came through from Oprah's office that she'd like us to do a house she'd picked exclusively for her show. So we dropped everything and flew to Chicago, where she's based. I'm not fazed by being on television and I've now appeared on countless chat shows, but appearing on Oprah's show was something special. It just seemed so ridiculous that a couple of years earlier I'd been earning £1,000 a month before tax working as someone's housekeeper, and now here I was sitting beside one of the most famous women in the world being beamed into millions of homes.

The woman whose house they'd chosen for Aggie and me to inspect and clean was an excellent subject. Carol had been married six times, always to wealthy men, and she'd had any amount of plastic surgery. Now in her late fifties, she was a very good-looking woman who lived in a lovely, airy house in a smart gated community in one of the Californian valleys. But the interior was like a pigsty.

I was pleased that Oprah's people had sourced the house for us. People often claim that we deliberately mess up the houses we visit; they can't believe that some people live like that. But they do, and having Oprah come up with a filthy house absolutely independently was proof that they do exist. It gave additional credibility to what we do.

Part of Carol's problem was depression. The failure of all those marriages and then the death of her mother had left her with little or no self-esteem. As she told Oprah, 'I felt like trash and I started to allow myself to live in trash.' You can say that again! When Aggie and I first went into her house it looked as though it had been burgled. But that was only its superficial appearance.

Carol had three dogs and two birds, and there were faeces and droppings everywhere. Laboratory tests showed that her toilet, though disgusting, was cleaner than the inside of her fridge. In the kitchen, Aggie found maggots crawling in a cooking pot that hadn't been opened and washed in two years. Initially I thought they were caked grains of rice – and then they started wriggling. Flies flew out of the fridge when you opened the door – there was meat putrefying on its shelves. There was more bacteria on the dining table, according to the results of a swab Aggie took, than in the average faeces. Truly, it was a Hammer House of Horrors.

And yet Carol was so beautifully turned out and so well-spoken. As Oprah pointed out, here was someone who had fundamental personality issues to sort out. She'd let herself – or, rather, her surroundings – deteriorate to the point where she didn't know how to begin to sort herself out. It took twenty-four hours to bag up fifty sacks of rubbish from inside her house. But the transformation was astonishing and Carol was determined, she said, not to let things slip ever again. 'This isn't a destination,' she told us, as she looked round her beautifully restored home. 'It's the beginning of a journey.'

Co-presenting *How Clean Is Your House?* has been a journey for Aggie and me, too. And we've come a long way in a short time. Since that first Channel 4 series in the early summer of 2003 our salary has soared, and we also now get well rewarded for appearing in advertisement campaigns, both in the UK and the USA. In the summer of 2005 I was able to buy a pretty house in Surrey and a nice car. We can afford to go on lovely holidays. After a lifetime of having to count the pennies, it seems incredible that my life could turn around so quickly.

The only downside I can think of is that I don't see as much of Pete as I'd like because I'm so busy. But this won't last for ever, and he supports me in this new career because we both know it will give us a lovely retirement. After my wretched start in life and my appalling first marriage it seems inconceivable that I should end up like this. No one has the right to say they're due a bit of good luck, but I can't help feeling that someone saw fit to smile on me at last. And I will say this. For the first time in my life, no one can mess with me. I've had too hard a life to take any more nonsense. I still maintain that, if I had the chance of living my life all over again and it included that brutal childhood, I'd rather not have been born.

It's to do with choices – or the lack of them. I had no choice but to be with my mother and she was a wicked, wicked woman. My darling son was taken from me. I found myself, first time round, married to a man who turned out to be an abusive womaniser. I had no alternative but to take a succession of poorly paid jobs. Well, I've had my fill of bad times. I'm never again going to have to do something I don't want to do because someone else has power over me. After all those years of struggling and making do, of merely surviving, I'm finally in the driving seat of my own life.

And that perhaps is the greatest prize of all.